New Directions in Educational Policy

THE PROFESSIONAL EDUCATION SERIES

Walter K. Beggs, *Editor*
Dean Emeritus
Teachers College
University of Nebraska

Royce H. Knapp, *Research Editor*
Regents Professor of Education
Teachers College
University of Nebraska

New Directions in
Educational Policy

by

John Martin Rich

School of Education
University of Texas at Austin

PROFESSIONAL EDUCATORS PUBLICATIONS, INC.
LINCOLN, NEBRASKA

Library of Congress Catalog Card No.: 73-92562

ISBN   0-88224-076-5

Contents

Preface

This is a book about educational policy. The basic reason for studying policy is that it significantly affects the lives of everyone. Each person, in his organizational and institutional roles, is embraced by a network of policy decisions that influence his behavior. Policies pervade organizational life, and since no one lives totally apart from social organizations, the impact of policy can scarcely be avoided.

My objectives are: (1) to provide a greater understanding of educational policy, and (2) to contribute to the improvement of policy-making. This book is addressed to laymen interested in the improvement of education, and to teachers and prospective teachers, administrators, other education specialists, and public officials.

In order to achieve the above objectives, I have attempted to show the importance of educational policy, its nature and sources, how it operates within its organizational setting, and how this setting can be improved. Finally, I have also attempted to show how policy is made, who makes it, and the possibilities for bringing about a new partnership among local, state, and federal levels.

I wish to thank Miss Karen Merkens for her efficient typing.

CHAPTER 1

The Importance of Policy

A sense of unrest and apprehension marks the present age; dissension and conflict are common features of our time. These tendencies are exacerbated by unprecedented social and technological changes in a period in which the rising expectations of many of the world's peoples are faced with sharply dwindling resources.

Institutions and organizations are also under attack. They have been accused of being "sick" bureaucracies which dehumanize and alienate, whose mechanisms are obsolescent for serving the ends they purport to fulfill.

Attacks against institutions may also at times represent attacks against policy. The reason for this is that policy constitutes the regulative mechanism for the daily operation of institutions. Dissatisfaction is expressed in many cases with the bureaucratic rules and "red tape" that tend to obstruct individuals in their relations with institutional personnel. Those desiring to secure employment or advancement within the system often complain about policies that seem to block them from achieving their purposes. But this is only one side of the coin. Policies can serve to facilitate organizational processes and ultimately aid in the organization's ability to attain its goals in the most efficacious manner. Policies may also structure an organization in such a way that human relations are enhanced and the quality of work is improved.

REASONS FOR STUDYING POLICY

The simplest and most basic reason for studying policy is that it has a significant effect on the lives of everyone. Each person has both a private and a public life; and it is in one's public life that policy exerts its effect. Policies interlace and pervade our institutional and organizational structures, and since no one lives his life totally apart from these structures, policy, for better or worse, will exercise its influence. Moreover, in the lives of many people who are part of the occupational world, day-to-day activities are regulated by policy. The quality of our organizations and their ability to fulfill their objectives are, in part, determined by basic policy decisions. Thus there are many reasons why the study of policy is an important undertaking.

With widespread criticism of institutions a characteristic feature of our times, no doubt there are those who hope that some institutions and organizations will fail to survive. But whether a group wishes to radically reconstruct institutions or innovate within them or preserve the status quo, it is essential that all groups focus on policy, for it lies at the very heart of organizational operations. A study of policy, in itself, does not commit one to take a particular position as to the purposes of institutional structures. Whatever one's attitudes toward institutional structures, one must first understand policy operations before he will be in a position to carry out his objectives.

There are those who believe—because of a conviction in the worth, say, of "participatory democracy"—that it is possible for organizations to be decentralized and have no formal leadership structure. Some may also think that policy would no longer be needed in such organizations. This is not the case, however. Even with a decentralized and a de-emphasized hierarchical arrangement, an organization would still utilize policy, although it might differ in function from policy in more traditional organizations.

THE SIGNIFICANCE OF POLICY IN EDUCATIONAL PRACTICE

All organizations and systems are regulated by policy, and educational systems are no exception. Policy not only regulates the internal operations of a system but also serves to regulate relationships and define functions among systems.

Policy is also important in the area of educational issues. Policy, by its very nature, can arouse controversy. This is due to the fact that policy statements establish a certain set of actions as appropriate in certain types of situations, thereby ruling out other possible actions.

Policy is also significant in terms of its relation to educational aims. Certain regulatory mechanisms are needed to control daily school operations in order that the system can attain its goals. At best, some form of regulation is a necessary but not a sufficient condition for goal fulfillment. Without regulation schools could scarcely be spoken of as a system, for in all systems there must be some means whereby the distinguishing relationships of the system are maintained over temporal periods. Through policy networks, orderly and predictable relationships are established and actions within the system can be referred to policy for interpretation and clarification.

A policy network also affects the ambience of a school system. That which is required, optional, or permissible is determinable by referring to the system's policy. The attitude of educational personnel and students toward school policy creates an atmosphere which may not always be easily definable but can be detected by a perceptive observer. This atmosphere conditions and reinforces the relationships that evolve and the satisfactions attained as a result of school experiences. The esprit de corps of a school system is considerably affected by policy, and the fact that some students feel they are being dehumanized stems in some cases from what they consider to be unjust policy decisions. Policies may foster or obstruct an effective learning atmosphere, they may promote good morale among students and faculty, or they may engender dissatisfaction and disaffection.

The teacher-learning process is both directly and indirectly affected by school policies. It is directly affected in a number of ways but most prominently in regulations and requirements for the curriculum and in policies that regulate and prescribe actions to be followed by teachers and students. Policy has an indirect effect upon the teacher-learning process by its influence on the ambience of the school and the subtle but pervasive ways in which classroom atmosphere and the attitudes of students toward learning and the schooling experience are affected.

THE STUDY OF POLICY

Up to the present the study of policy itself has had a certain ambiguity and lack of completeness. It is not the case that researchers have ignored the area of policy or failed to recognize its importance; rather, the policy research conducted has been limited to certain areas and thereby has failed to answer many essential questions. Probably the areas most neglected are the nature of policy, its source and justification, and how policy-making can be improved. These are also some of the most fundamental areas, and consequently their neglect leads to an incomplete understanding of policy itself. Additionally, even though other areas have been explored with varying degrees of thoroughness and sophistication, these studies would be more fully informed if they could draw with greater confidence upon all areas of policy study.

There are a number of important studies of policy operations in their institutional setting. These studies have focused, however, not primarily on policy per se but on organizational systems, applying various models from organizational theory.[1] Other investigators have concerned themselves with human-relations factors and the means whereby organizations can become less dehumanizing.[2] And there also have been explorations of the school as a bureaucratic system.[3]

Discussion of policy matters in these and cognate studies has been within the context of an organizational system—and rightfully so, for policy does not operate within a vacuum but in a social context. Although it is possible to isolate the individuals who make key decisions, a full understanding of the process can only be gained by viewing it relationally within an organizational setting. These studies tend to concentrate on theories and models of bureaucracy, role-playing, factors contributing to control and innovation within the system. Policy is studied as one facet of organizational operations rather than being singled out as the central focus for such studies. Even though such studies do not usually reveal how policy is derived or justified, they do convey how it operates in organizational settings.

There have also been a number of case studies of the formation and implementation of educational policy at the local, state, and federal levels.[4] Although these studies are diverse, many of them have concentrated on certain aspects of educational decision-making and the use of political power.

Case studies of the political process at the different levels have been valuable in promoting a better understanding of the development and implementation of policy within the larger context of politics and the uses of power. These studies have enabled educators to gain a more realistic understanding of these processes and contributed to the development of more sophisticated political skills. Although many of these studies offer a critical as well as a descriptive dimension, they usually fail to develop any ideal models for policy which can be used to evaluate actual policy decisions.

There also are empirical and historical studies of policy decisions on educational issues. The issues are diverse and include church-state relations, academic freedom, loyalty, and others.[5] These studies generally help provide perspective on the genesis of the issue, the conflicting parties involved, and the educational consequences of various policy decisions.

Policy studies have been conducted in a number of other disciplines.[6] These studies may shed some light on education in those instances where generic similarities exist in basic policy considerations.

Occasionally there have been inquiries into the nature and function of policy; more frequently case studies have been undertaken to determine how policy is established and implemented in business organizations, on matters of trade relations with other nations, foreign aid, urban mass transportation systems, and other areas.

In many investigations, however, although policy is discussed, it remains somewhat peripheral. In political science, policy is one among a number of topics related to studies of power, legislation, and other focal areas. In the study of organizations, policy is of secondary consideration to organizational models, conceptions of bureaucracy, authority, and role-playing. In educational administration, policy is almost invariably considered to be of importance, but it is not usually given primary attention. The same state of affairs generally holds in other areas, such as public administration and business. Thus there is a need for studies devoted exclusively to policy and its operations within an institutional setting.

AN OVERVIEW OF THE BOOK

There have been a number of misconceptions of the nature of policy, leading a number of investigators to report a set of phenomena as matters of policy when such matters are actually not policy at all. To help rectify this difficulty, the next chapter is devoted to the nature of policy, for policy studies surely cannot advance very far as long as researchers not only hold divergent conceptions of policy but also confuse policy with other institutional outcomes and operations. Goals, norms, traditions, decisions, and issues are likely to be confused with policy or, in some way, equated with policy, The similarities and differences between policy and these other factors, processes, or outcomes are distinguished in the next chapter.

Once policy is more clearly delineated, we can turn our attention, in Chapter 3, to the source of policy decisions. There are certain basic problems in the formulation of policy. Probably the most obdurate problem is the source(s) from which policy may be derived. Since the derivation of policy should not be fortuitous or arbitrary, there should be ample consideration of the various sources available to policy-makers.

Policy can be isolated for purposes of study, but it must be remembered that policy is an integral part of institutions and their operations. In Chapter 4, policy is examined within its institutional setting in terms of the operations of bureaucracies and their influences on policy. The process of changing bureaucratic school systems is explored in terms of the effect this would have on policy.

The final chapter examines how policy is actually made, and then offers proposals for the improvement of this process. Next, the question, Who makes policy? is explored in terms of local school districts. The outside influences on local policy-making—state, regional, federal, and national—are also discussed. Finally, an exploration is made of proposals for new relationships among these levels.

CHAPTER 2

The Nature of Policy

Before undertaking a more complete investigation of policy operations in educational institutions, it is first necessary to clarify the nature of policy. In this chapter we will show the relationship of policy to rules, tradition, decisions, general norms, and issues. Additionally, the stages of policy development will be examined. Prior to these undertakings, however, some common misconceptions of policy will be discussed.

MISCONCEPTIONS CONCERNING THE NATURE OF POLICY

Some definitions of policy or policy-making are tendentious. The National Academy of Education states that "policy making, almost by definition, is the conscious attempt of officials, legislators, and interested publics, to find constructive responses to the needs and pathologies which they observe in their surrounding culture."[1]

This definition tells us not only who should participate in policy-making ("officials, legislators, and interested publics"), but also the ends which policy-making should strive to fulfill ("find constructive responses to the needs and pathologies which they observe in their surrounding culture"). As for participants in policy-making, presumably teachers would not be among them; although the term *interested publics* could cover heterogeneous groups in the nation at large, teachers are not expressly mentioned.

To find "constructive responses to the needs and pathologies" observed in the larger culture would imply that the act of policy-making is designed to ameliorate certain conditions as opposed to stabilizing and maintaining existing relations. In this sense the definition is prescriptive, insofar as it recommends that policy-making should aim to bring about certain changes rather than reinforce existing arrangements. This prescriptive form would differ from an empirical approach, which states essentially what the policy-maker actually does.

15

One difficulty with definitions of the prescriptive type is that they are largely hortatory in tone, urging policy-makers to act in one way rather than another. Unfortunately, the definition offers very little understanding of the policy-making process, for it would be possible to substitute for the words *policy-making* such terms as *planning, innovation,* or *decision-making* and make just as much sense. In other words, the definition is far too general and nebulous to distinguish policy-making from other related processes, and, therefore, the definition is not very useful for advancing inquiry.

Policy has at times been linked to goals and purposes. Roald F. Campbell and his associates use the term *policy* to mean "the expression of the broad goals or purposes of education."[2] Other writers have considered policy in a similar manner. John Walton, for instance, uses the term *policy formation* to mean "the setting up of the purposes of an organization, making choices between conflicting purposes, and modifying established purposes."[3]

In order to see why these definitions are misinterpretations of policy or policy-making, it is necessary, first of all, to be clear as to what is meant by goals, purposes, or aims. The source of aims is a philosophy of education or a value system. This does not mean that empirical factors are ignored. Educators must assess existing conditions and practices along with the resources available before they can realistically propose a set of aims or goals. Aims express values; they express that which is prized, thought valuable and desirable. The process of establishing aims consists first of formulating them clearly and in such a manner that their fulfillment can be evaluated. Secondly, there is the justification stage: defensible reasons should be developed for espousing one set of aims rather than another. Thus, even if aims are stated clearly and are amenable to evaluation, one can always ask for a justification for the choice of a particular set of aims. The function of aims is to give a sense of direction to the educational process, provide purposefulness to educators and learners, and offer a way of evaluating educational programs.

The function of policy, however, differs from that of aims. Policy essentially serves to regulate institutions and organizations; it provides orderly procedures for day-by-day operations and thereby affords a sense of continuity. Policy is also used to specify the allocation of funds and resources to a project, to establish guidelines for the conduct of programs, and to state what is prescribed, prohibited, or permitted in a social system.

There are numerous ways in which these different functions can be illustrated. Policy, as we will see later, takes the form of a covering rule applicable to a cluster of similar cases that fall under the rule. The rules and regulations that govern the operations of organizations can be considered to be forms of policy. Policies also serve to regulate the allocation of resources to projects and programs by specifying the rules governing such operations. Thus policies have a pervasive quality since personnel are directly affected by policy in their daily assignments. Policy also provides a set of expectations and directives that relate to the roles of individuals in the organization. In order to fulfill their roles successfully (at least from the administration's point of view), they are expected to comply with the system's policies. Policy, in this sense, prescribes or prohibits certain behavior. Policy may also state the areas of behavior that are not regulated; but in many cases the individual usually assumes that where policy fails to specify responsibilities, one is free to choose for himself (assuming that organizational folklore or the "grapevine" does not suggest otherwise).

Even though policy can and should be distinguished from goals or aims, this does not mean that they are unrelated or have little significance for one another. Actually, if policy is genuinely effective, it will aid the system in achieving its aims. An unregulated system, lacking guidelines for its daily operations, could scarcely expect to attain its goals. Of course it always is possible, though not very likely, that a system could realize its goals by accident, but no official would be likely to leave such an important matter to chance. The exact nature of the relation between goals and policies shall be discussed in greater detail later but it is sufficient to emphasize at this point that an important connection exists, between goals and policies.

Some authors attempt to distinguish policy from other actions which have a family resemblance to it. Raymond Bauer, for instance, distinguishes between routine actions, tactical decisions, and policy.[4] Routine actions, he claims, demand little cogitation, are repetitive and trivial; tactical decisions are more complex, demand greater thought, and have wider ramifications; whereas policy has the widest ramifications, the longest time perspective, and demands the most information and cognition.

But Bauer also recognizes the limitation of such distinctions by noting that what is policy for one person may be tactics for another. This he illustrates by pointing out that when the superintendent of a factory sends a directive to a foreman, the directive becomes policy for the foreman, who, in turn, formulates "tactical" decisions, which become policy for his workers.[5] Thus, what is policy depends upon the perspective of the individual involved and, therefore, although it may be possible to distinguish routine actions, the difference between tactical decisions and policy may depend upon individual perspective. Moreover, to restrict policy to actions that have the widest ramifications, as does Bauer, would ignore the many policies which regulate the daily operations of organizations. For example, in every school system there are a host of policies that regulate student behavior and provide guidelines on the use of school equipment and the maintenance of the school plant. Any one of these policies by itself lacks wide ramification, but, taken together, they do exert considerable influence over the operation of the system.

POLICY AND RULES

Policy can be better understood as a form of rule. A rule is a type of generalization used to prescribe conduct, action, or usage. The function of policy within an institution is "to regulate (to bring under rule) decision-behavior on matters of concern to the institution."[6] As social relations become increasingly complex, it is necessary that formal regulations be established to govern actions so as to avoid unnecessary disputes and conflicts. There is also a need to render actions more predictable so that institutions can operate in an orderly manner. Thus, rules are established to regulate institutions and bring about a greater degree of predictability in institutional processes.

By following a rule one's action is said to be rule-governed. A rule may provide general instructions as to what one should do in order to fulfill an objective. There are numerous rules that provide general instructions: rules of chess, cooking, sewing, driving a car, and so forth. Other rules regulate one's relations to persons or property: for example, rules regulating lining up to receive instructions, running in the hall, walking on the grass.

A significant part of early socialization is to teach children about rules and require them to obey certain rules. It is only when the child grows older that he no longer believes rules are sacrosanct. Piaget, in studying the game of marbles, found that there are several stages in the child's conception of rules.[7] In the earliest stage, rules grow out of the child's neuromuscular development. Between the ages of two and five, the child imitates the rules of others without trying to win. Rules at this stage are considered sacred and eternal. A less egocentric and more social outlook develops between the ages of seven and eight. The child now tries to win, and he shows concern for the mutual unification and control of rules, although his ideas about them are somewhat vague. Between the ages of eleven and twelve, the rules of the game have become fixed and a high level of agreement exists among the players. Children now recognize that rules are formed by mutual consent and that a majority can agree to change the rules. It is at this age that the child's conception of rules resembles that of an adult.

The point of this apparent digression about the child's evolving conception of rules relates not only to the behavior that teachers can expect of children and youth in this area but to adult behavior as well. The adult's ability to respond intelligently to rules is behavior which is learned. The individual's earlier training enables him to understand what it means to obey a rule.

Rules are usually stated in the imperative mood ("Grades in each course are due [must be turned in] forty-eight hours after the final exam" or "No running in the halls"). Rules seemingly imply some external authority who formulates and issues them, even though persons who follow them may actually have participated in their formulation. However, if all the rules of a school system are formulated by an authority or authorities—say, the superintendent and the school board—they probably will not be obeyed indefinitely unless, in the experience of the personnel, they have some justification in experience.

Rules justify themselves in experience when they help to secure a desired end and when they do so efficiently. However, it is not always the case that a desired end can be achieved by following a single rule, since in some cases the observance of a number of related rules over a period of time may be necessary to achieve the desired outcome (as in the case of learning).

In the matter of efficiency, rule A is preferred to B in order to achieve end E if A can achieve E more efficiently and not create contraindicative side-effects. For example, although there may be several drugs which, properly administered, can overcome a particular disease, a physician may know that one drug is preferable to the others, based on clinical evidence, because it is known to cure the disease more quickly and before it has time to move into its later, more serious stages. In this case the physician would apply the rule to use drug A rather than B or C to achieve the end E (cure the disease) as long as there are no contraindications. If the patient has serious allergies to drug A but no allergies to drugs B and C, then one of the latter drugs will be chosen, based on its availability and its known therapeutic effects.

In applying this formula to education, one must also consider efficiency and side-effects. Rule A is superior to B in order to achieve end E if A can achieve E more efficiently with no greater side-effects. In the matter of efficiency in learning, speed, parsimony, retention of learned materials, minimum expenditure of resources, and other factors may be considered. There are a host of undesirable side-effects, however. Of the more general kind, those that create an antipathy in students toward a particular subject or dehumanize and alienate are sufficiently serious to contraindicate using a particular approach or following a certain rule. In view of the present status of our knowledge of the educational process, it is not possible in many cases to predict with much sense of certainty the probable outcome of following one rule (or set of rules) rather than another.

Rule-governed behavior—as opposed to capricious behavior or blindly following a routine—can be thought of as rational in the sense that reasons can be offered: reasons can be given for abiding by a rule in terms of its ability to achieve the desired end and its efficacy in doing so. Dispute at this point could arise over whether the claims for the rule can be supported. The dispute is settled by reference to authoritative case studies which demonstrate that following the rule achieves the stated objectives. In cases where such evidence is unavailable, acting on the rule must then be tested sufficiently in experience to determine the possible outcomes.

Another type of dispute questions the ends that rule-following is designed to fulfill. This is not a case, however, where the rules are in doubt, for it could be openly admitted by all parties to the dispute that the rules chosen achieve the ends more efficiently than any other set of rules. Since the ends are in dispute, the question of the appropriateness of the rules and the reasonableness of following them is put aside until the questions about ends are successfully adjudicated.

Thus, since policy takes the form of a covering rule, an understanding of the nature, operations, and use of rules provides an initial understanding of the nature and basis of policy.

NORMATIVE ASPECTS OF POLICY-MAKING

Policy-making has both normative and empirical dimensions. The empirical side, which is not uncommonly considered the more basic side, consists, from the point of view of those who study policy, of the actual operations used by policy-makers in developing and implementing policy decisions. Such studies report what is done and seek out common features of policy-making situations in order to arrive at grounded generalizations about policy-making. The observer also looks for situations which pose policy questions and promotes the reconsideration of existing policies and the proposal of new ones. Another area of interest is that of determining who makes policy. Such investigations may seek to uncover whether community policy-making is conducted by a power elite or by a plurality of different groups. Finally, for those who believe that policy-making consists of certain skills which can be taught, different theories are advanced as to the nature of these skills. Does policy-making consist primarily of problem-solving, data-gathering, value adjudication, futuristic thinking, or planning strategies, or of some combination of these and other skills and abilities? Presumably, once the essential features of policy-making are delineated, leaders can be taught how to improve their skills. Apparently policy-making has certain fundamental characteristics irrespective of the institutional setting.

As stated earlier, one of the chief functions of policy is to regulate. To regulate a social system means that certain classes of actions are prescribed. It is important to note that, for the most part, policy regulates "classes of actions" rather than specific acts. The number of specific acts performed by the total personnel of an organization of any size is enormous, and it would not be in the interest of policy-makers to attempt through the policy-making mechanisms to bring them all under some form of regulation. There are many minor acts which it is not in the interest of the organization to regulate—from tying one's shoes to the exchange of greetings. Moreover, since it may be necessary to regulate any number of acts that are not identical, it is necessary to state policy in such a manner that it takes the form of a covering rule. In other words, a single policy covers a number of related actions. This is the case, for instance, of policies regulating the functions and responsibilities of personnel. One cannot sum up the acts needed or state that acts performed in a certain sequence constitute the fulfillment of policies governing the performance. The appraisal is usually based on certain overall performances that result in desired outcomes. The quality of the performance would be evaluated in terms of a set of standards; the general functions to be performed would be prescribed by policy.

The fact of regulating and, hence, prescribing is a normative characteristic of the use of policy. To use language for the purpose of prescribing or evaluating is to be engaged in normative discourse. Policy statements generally take the following form: "One ought to do X in circumstance(s) (or situations) C." For example, in stating the functions of the superintendent of schools, policy statements may also be made: "The superintendent shall serve as the chief executive officer of the board of education and chief educational adviser to the board. In this capacity the superintendent will be expected to apprise the board of all important policy matters, to utilize his professional knowledge in board deliberations, and to faithfully execute board policy." As noted in the above example, a policy statement does not attempt to state the numerous actions necessary for the superintendent in order to fulfill the functions with which he has been charged, but on the basis of evidence supplied by the superintendent and other parties, the board will be in a position to evaluate the extent to which the superintendent has successfully implemented prescribed policies. The evaluation is made with reference to a set of standards used to appraise the superintendent's performance.

Thus, policy has an "ought" or "should" dimension which renders its operation normative. All policies have prescriptive force. The person(s) to whom the policy applies has the choice of following or not following the policy; but if he is an employee and wishes to advance, it is likely that he will abide by the policy. Organizations, however, increase the prescriptive force of policy by employing a system of sanctions. The organization, ideally speaking, provides the highest rewards to those who abide by established policy and whose performance achieves the highest standards; whereas those who fail to comply with policy and whose performance-level is low, fail to advance in the system and may be discharged. (This description, however, would apply only to a meritocratic system.) It is possible, when policies and goals are not properly coordinated with one another (as is sometimes the case in large-scale organizations), that an employee may not follow certain policies but still facilitate goal attainment. In such cases the individual may still be penalized if policy compliance is judged to be good in itself; but in a more flexible organization his facilitation of goals despite failure to comply may result in a reappraisal of policy.

Sometimes an employee may fail to carry out a policy, not from unwillingness or disobedience, but because it lies beyond his capacity. There are several possible reasons for this: the individual is not the right person for the job; the policy is unreasonable; the job requirements have recently changed and the individual has not yet developed the new skills needed. A policy might be considered unreasonable if it demands far more of an employee than could be reasonably demanded of others, in view of their requisite skills and abilities, in the same job classification. A policy is not efficacious when it leads away from or impedes the attainment of stated goals. It is therefore "unreasonable" to ask employees to comply with such policies.

A policy recommends an act or series of acts; it has prescriptive force. Policy statements do not offer reasons, but it is not improper for those who are expected to fulfill a policy to ask for reasons. In other words, policies are not arbitrary or based on whim or caprice. That they have been officially approved by the organization gives them a sense of legitimacy and prescriptive force. But since the policy network of an organization (its totality of policy statements) is formulated to advance the organization or, with some organizations, to promote the welfare of its members, one can rightfully ask for the reasons which led to the formulation of a particular policy whenever the policy seems unreasonable or nonefficacious. Thus policies differ in this respect from commands because wherever one is part of a system where it is legitimate to be commanded, one is not in a position to ask for reasons why he should obey.

By its regulative function policy aids the organization in attaining its goals. It would be somewhat inaccurate to claim that policy provides the means that are used to attain organizational goals; more accurately, policy provides the normative framework within which various means become operative. These means may be prescribed or, if not explicitly prohibited, permitted. The policy network also provides strategies and guidelines for organizational operations. But it is a mistake to consider the formulation of ends and the formulation of policy as having a strong normative dimension while regarding the determination of means as an empirical matter. John Walton, for example, argues that where there is consensus on ends, the determination of means is essentially an empirical matter.[8] To follow this line of reasoning, however, leads to a separation of means and ends. Efficiency and efficacy, although not to be ignored, are alone insufficient to determine appropriate means. It is necessary, for instance, to consider side-effects upon students and teachers in the choice of means and the evaluation of these side-effects in terms of their desirability, which is largely a normative operation. It is not uncommon that certain bureaucratic practices, which become means, may be the most efficient and efficacious to employ, especially when the ends are limited in scope; but to ignore the side-effects, as has been the case in some school systems, may result in justifiable claims that the means are dehumanizing. It is also generally agreed that means and ends must be consonant; therefore, it is indefensible to use undemocratic means to achieve democratic ends. The determination of what means are democratic is not only an empirical matter but a normative one as well.

POLICY AND TRADITION

In older school systems, faculty and students may observe traditions that have been formed over the years. The observance of these traditions, in addition to its other functions, may bring about greater regularity and predictability in human relations. Traditions tend to provide structure to social interaction by defining appropriate responses and modes of behavior. They also remove much of the element of chance and idiosyncratic behavior found in relations that are unregulated. Thus tradition and policy have the generic similarity of providing structure and regularity to social relations. In this sense, tradition and policy fulfill some of the same functions.

It could be said, however, that while tradition remains largely unexamined, policy is frequently reexamined and modified. This is generally the case, although social systems of both past and present have treated certain policies as sacrosanct. Nonetheless, tradition is generally treated more uncritically than policy.

There may be cases where tradition is critically examined and accepted as a desirable way to continue regulating a certain aspect of institutional operation. At the point where such decisions are formulated and agreed upon, they become a matter of policy.

One of the chief differences between policy and tradition is that policy is deliberately and consciously developed. Thus the very fact that institutional leaders consider it necessary to develop policy is a clear indication that traditions and customs are insufficient to perform the full range of policy functions. While some traditions may be consistent and supportive of the policy network, others may tend to preclude the effective operation of the system. For instance, certain traditions within the school and the larger community have impeded policies regulating the desegregation of schools. In another area, long-standing traditions sanctioning Bible reading and the recitation of prayers in public schools have conflicted with policies formulated in accordance with Supreme Court decisions prohibiting an "establishment of religion."

Traditions and customs interlace all institutions and exert varying degrees of persuasive force over their members; and the very fact that traditions and customs may facilitate or impede existing policies, is all the more reason why an assessment of institutional operations must give careful attention to the effects of tradition.

When a set of traditions obstructs the fulfillment of policy, institutional leaders may employ various tactics to overcome the resistance. The most common approach, after informing personnel about policy and its implications, is to apply sanctions: reward those who observe policy and penalize those who fail to do so. This tactic works best among those who identify with the system, consider its demands legitimate, and desire the rewards and advancements which the system has to offer. Institutional leaders strive to gain such commitment among personnel. Those lacking such commitment are viewed either as unsuitable organizational members who should be discharged if their behavior does not improve quickly, or as members for whom the indoctrination process has failed. In the latter case, the usual tactic is to proceed with reindoctrination; in some instances leaders may first examine indoctrination processes to determine whether they are deficient in some way before proceeding with reindoctrination. The indoctrination process, common to all organizations but varying in content, is the means by which new members are socialized to their roles and organizational expectations.

Another approach to overcoming the resistance of tradition is by demythologizing the tradition. Among those who consider certain traditions sacrosanct, sanctions and further indoctrination may not always prove effective because of guilt associated with violating the particular tradition. Long-standing traditions often gain support from the myths with which they are surrounded. By demythologizing the tradition it is robbed of its compelling nature for those whose attachment rests on these grounds. But since belief in myth is not rationally based, the undermining of myths by rational argument or empirical evidence is not likely to completely demythologize traditions. Thus, the surrogation of the function performed by the traditon, through the performance of new activities which are consonant with policy and provide the needed emotional support, is the most likely means in this case of replacing the tradition-oriented behavior and enabling the individual to accept demythologizing the tradition.

DECISIONS, POLICIES, AND GENERAL NORMS

Decisions and general norms are likely to be confused with policies. R. Bruce Raup and his associates have made a distinction between decisions, policies, and general norms, which they refer to as types of practical judgment.[9]

Decisions, the first type of practical judgment, pertain to what one should do in a particular state of affairs without regard for reconstructing generalizations to guide future conduct. In making decisions, one determines what should be done in a particular case without developing generalizations that apply to other cases of a similar type. One may decide on the basis of a principle or by the use of common sense.

Raup considers policy as providing a stabilizing plan which provides consistency from one case to another. Decisions arise when some exception is established which requires the abandonment or reconstruction of policy.

General norms emerge from the value system of a culture. They serve as the moral principles and ideals by means of which the general rules of conduct are constructed. When policy-making is undergirded by general norms, it provides a broader social context for its development.

Another distinction can be made between policy and general norms. Stanley E. Ballinger suggests that although both policy and norms serve to regulate, general or regulative norms are relatively universal and noncontextual in their scope.[10] In other words, they apply equally to persons in various situations and circumstances; they are stated as universals. Thus a prohibition against murder applies to everyone. On the other hand, policies are context-dependent because they regulate the activities and operations of a particular institution, or subunit of an institution, at a certain time and place. Policies, in contrast to general norms, apply to a given group of personnel whose actions fall within the framework of the regulative scope of a particular policy. Thus the study of general or regulative norms is investigated by sociology and anthropology as an empirical study, and in the field of ethics as a study of right conduct. It can therefore be seen that investigations in policy formation differ considerably from those which focus on general norms.

The relation of policy and decisions, however, is more complex than Raup indicates. This is principally due to the development of decision-making theory and the claim that it can be used as the basis for policy-making. Investigators in decision-making theory are concerned with those aspects of human behavior in which choices are made among alternatives. Criteria are developed for determining the relative importance of goals and the probable efficiency of different alternatives in achieving the desired goal. The descriptive dimension of the field studies how decisions are made; whereas the normative dimension develops models of how decisions should be made and how decision-making can be improved. Decision-making has been approached, through empirical studies by social and behavioral scientists, by examining the processes by which decisions are made, the source of decisions within organizations, and the consequences of decisions. Others concerned with the improvement of decision-making frequently use a mathematical approach known as "statistical decision theory." According to Irwin Bross, this type of theory not only utilizes statistics but draws ideas from cost accounting, theory of games, information theory, economics, and logic.[11] The work on mathematical models utilizes theory of games,[12] and the mathematical side has frequently drawn from Bayesian statistics.[13] There is also a close relation between some of the work in industry known as "operations research" and decision-making theory, particularly in the use of mathematical models.[14]

A cornerstone of decision-making theory is the objective of determining the best course of action in a given situation. The theory seeks to find the most efficient and effective course of action among the various alternatives in a situation; thus it attempts to develop a system for making optimal decisions. Decision-making theory, according to C. West Churchman, is "an attempt to find criteria for selecting 'optimal' decisions among a set of alternative actions—where optimality is based . . . on some measure of the values of various outcomes that may result from selecting each of the actions."[15]

Herbert A. Simon, however, has argued that the maximizing model is unrealistic and inappropriate in terms of human behavior. He contends that "economic man is a *satisficing* animal whose problem solving is based on search activity to meet certain aspiration levels rather than a *maximizing* animal whose problem solving involves finding the best alternatives in terms of specified criteria."[16] In other words, it is not possible for the decision-maker to assess the multiplicity of variables and the numerous possible alternatives in a complex decision. What usually occurs is a search for an alternative that will reasonably satisfy one's aspiration level at a given time.

Decision-makers may act irrationally—fail to act in terms of the best estimate of costs, gains, and probabilities, or conduct a faulty evaluation of these factors in terms of the available evidence. Moreover, the presence of unconscious or partly conscious motives, while not invalidating decision-making theory, poses formidable difficulties. In terms of predicting decision, it would first be necessary to know something about motivating factors, and a rational model of decision-making does not provide a way to account for them. It has been suggested by Martin Patchen that decision-making theory be supplemented by motivational theory so that dispositions toward action and various incentives can be assessed.[17]

Thus it can be seen that at present there are certain basic problems in decision-making theory that limit the realization of its objectives. Additionally, since there are fundamental differences between decisions and policies, which were noted earlier, it would be somewhat misleading and self-defeating to employ decision-making theory as the primary model for policy formation.

POLICY AND EDUCATIONAL ISSUES

A policy is not an issue, although it is not uncommon for policies to generate issues as a result of the reaction of those who in some way are affected. An educational issue occurs whenever two or more contrasting or conflicting educational positions are publicly expressed and debated, and the outcome is likely to affect an educational system or systems in terms of major policy decisions.

For an issue to occur there must first be differences of position, for no issue exists where consensus reigns. A position can be taken on any number of educational matters—federal aid to education, religious instruction in public schools, busing, and censorship of reading materials, to cite a few examples. These differences cannot be so slight that no dispute arises: the positions must sharply contrast with one another or conflict before an issue begins to germinate. The issue must be publicly expressed and debated before it is possible to arouse concerted group action; it cannot be strictly a private matter if it is to engender public awareness and concern. An issue becomes significant when the disposition of it is likely to affect an educational system or systems in terms of certain major policy decisions.

It is not a simple matter to distinguish major policy decisions from minor ones, because, as noted earlier, the determination of what is major or minor rests with the observer and his perception of how the policy affects him. It might be thought that policies regulating taking, recording, and reporting attendance are minor policies relative to more far-reaching policies such as those which regulate admission practices in segregated school districts. However, from the point of view of some teachers, the attendance policies may be considered to be major ones. Examining a school system from the perspective of a qualified independent observer, however, there is little question that the admissions policies would be regarded as of major importance. Should the attendance policies generate issues which have impact upon the major policies of a school system, then it is likely, depending upon the outcome of the issues, that attendance policies will assume major importance during the period when these issues are at their height.

Policy decisions may generate issues, and issues may affect policies. The establishment of a policy sanctioning a teacher-led prayer before the beginning of classes each day may crystallize positions in the community pitting those who contend that the practice violates the Supreme Court decision and those who believe that religion is the basis of morality and democracy and its teachings cannot be left to chance. The policy authorizing the busing of students to overcome racial imbalance may also arouse issues, notably among those who are opposed to busing for such purposes and those who support it (whatever the underlying reasons of both parties). Thus the establishment of new policies always increases the likelihood that issues will arise. But educators should not take the attitude that issues should be avoided at all costs, for the very fact that issues exist is an accurate indication that certain segments of the community are not apathetic. After periods of strife, quiescent intervals are greatly welcomed; but long periods of apathy and noninvolvement among community members are not a healthy sign. Controversy is aroused by the very nature of an issue. It is only when an issue reaches the point of intense conflict among the concerned parties that it becomes counterproductive and divisive and may thereby lead to an undermining of certain vital aspects of the educational system.

Issues affect policies through the process of public discussion and debate over the issues; from these discussions an administrator may conclude that the net effects of a new set of policies will fail to achieve the intended results. The policies can continue to be fought for, or they may be rescinded. But when policies fail to secure the results sought, the usual tactic is to strike the policies and initiate new, more promising ones. Thus policy matters are always open to change and reevaluation, and since the outcomes resulting from a policy, rather than a particular policy itself, are valued, policy-makers must remain sufficiently open, receptive, and experimental to make the necessary changes. The tendency to value a set of policies for their own sake comes about by the association of a given set of policies with a certain outcome, leading to the belief that no other set of policies can achieve the desired results. This may very well be a true belief, but it cannot be corroborated without providing sufficient evidence in its support. Considering the complexity of school systems and the multiple variables involved in their operation, it would be misleading to believe that only one set of policies can achieve a desired result.

Except in the case of private dissatisfaction clandestine actions to undermine policies which are opposed, attacks on policies arise out of educational issues. These issues may already be present when a new set of policies is passed. When the policies serve to heighten debate and controversy to the level of open conflict, there is a real danger that the policies will be undermined. On the other hand, some new policies do not impinge on existing issues and are likely to remain publicly unopposed until new issues arise which bear directly upon the policies.

Of course, policies may also be abolished not only as a result of conflicts aroused by issues but because of the common problem that they are simply unworkable. No doubt issues may be incited by unworkable policies that leaders attempt to maintain at all costs, but there are a number of unworkable policies that fail to generate issues. This tendency may be due either to the fact that new policies are promptly substituted when the failure of the old ones becomes evident (thereby undercutting protracted conflict), or because the policies are minor ones and fail to arouse deep or widespread concern.

This is not to say that one should always look to issues in order to explain the development of new policies. Actually, new policies can arise from a change in the philosophy of a school system, its goals, priorities, values, or as a result of financial exigencies or a reorganization of programs and operating procedures. Some of these factors will be discussed more fully in the next chapter.

STAGES OF POLICY DEVELOPMENT

At this point, the stages of policy development will be overviewed, and they will be explored more thoroughly in subsequent chapters. The stages of policy development are: formulation, dissemination, implementation, and evaluation.

The formulation stage assumes a source or sources from which new policy can be derived. Among the sources are philosophy, science, value systems, educational aims, educational standards, public opinion, and futuristic studies. In Chapter 3 these sources, in terms of their value and limitations, will be examined in detail. For the present it is important to note that policy-makers should have some basis for deriving policy prior to reaching decisions on the policies chosen and their final form. The reliance on sources assures a solid base for policy development (assuming the source is a fruitful one) and provides a sense of direction and continuity between past policies and the development of new ones. This is made possible by utilizing the same source(s) each time that new policies must be developed. Furthermore, a source provides a rationale or justification for policy by enabling the policy-maker to show that his actions are not arbitrary, capricious, or expedient—in other words, that there is a rational basis for his action. Whether the source is entirely adequate or appropriate is another question. The point is that there are relatively independent bases from which policy can be derived and which can be appealed to when policies are questioned.

Once general decisions have been made as to the types of policies needed, the matter of formulation arises. Policy statements range from highly general to very specific. The grading policies of a school are usually stated in specific terms, whereas policies pertaining to equal opportunity may be stated in general terms. In the latter case the statement may affirm an "open admissions" policy. This leaves the policy open to interpretation in light of the circumstances and situation.

On the one hand, the general terms in which it is formulated provide flexibility and the ability to adapt it to changing situations; on the other hand, they may make it susceptible to limited or distorted interpretations. But the very fact that some policies must be written to cover multiple and even unpredictable situations renders it essential that policy statements of this type be formulated in sufficiently broad and flexible terms.

It is generally assumed that policies should always be formulated clearly and unambiguously. However, there are cases where the only way in which support of a policy can be gained is to formulate it in equivocal terms. Each of the contending groups can thereby read into the policy some way by which the policy will be beneficial to it or its constituents. Problems may arise at the implementation stage when one or more of the groups discovers that the execution of the policy has untoward tendencies and directions which are not likely to accrue the benefits anticipated. Nonetheless, the determination of the desirability of a policy and its continuation cannot be based strictly on its formulation but must also consider its outcomes.

After a new policy or set of policies is formulated, it is necessary that it be disseminated to all parties expected to carry it out and to those who will in some way be affected. When new policies are complex or involve new ways of behavior among institutional members, it may be necessary to lay the groundwork for such changes through conferences and discussions in addition to the more formal channels of communication. Moreover, new policies will occasionally clash with pockets of vested interests, which compounds the task of the policy-maker. He must anticipate some of the resistances to change prior to disseminating policy in order to overcome, compensate for, or pacify these forces. In other cases, it may be necessary to interpret complex and far-reaching policy decisions by a series of guidelines which make explicit the steps needed to execute the policy. Thus, in the dissemination stage the policy-maker must anticipate and evaluate a host of factors prior to deciding on the proper course of action; such factors as the complexity of the policy changes, the degree to which the policy breaks with past practices, the ability of personnel to execute the policy successfully, and the possible conflict of the policy with vested interests are all matters that merit careful assessment in determining dissemination procedures.

The process of dissemination relates closely to the next stage, which is known as implementation, or execution. Policies cannot be successfully implemented when personnel are not adequately informed or when they fail to understand their role in policy implementation. The implementation of policy can be better understood in terms of the effect on organizational roles. In order for personnel who are charged with implementing new policies to do so successfully, it is first necessary for them to reconceptualize their role by internalizing their new responsibilities and relating them to existing ones. To implement a policy successfully one not only has to be able to grasp its meaning and ramifications, but also must determine what types of actions are most likely to fulfill the policy. In order to execute policy successfully, standards of successful performance are needed, otherwise one would have no idea whether his execution is a success or failure. Determining the degree of success or failure is usually not a difficult problem with the more specific policies. For instance, policies that regulate grading are usually sufficiently definite and precise that the individual can know almost immediately whether his performance complies with the policies. On the other hand, policies pertaining to equal educational opportunity, such as racial balancing, busing, and admissions, are oftentimes formulated with sufficient generality that they can be employed to cover a number of situations. The more general policy statement is often made necessary by the need to provide flexibility in the face of rapidly changing social conditions, school populations, legislation, and guidelines.

Because of the facts that systematic policy studies have a very short history, that the variables to be assessed are multiple and usually uncontrolled, and that there is no widespread agreement on the methodology of policy evaluation, the stage of evaluation has yet to be developed in the policy literature. A general systems approach to evaluation would attempt to determine the new output of a system by ascertaining inputs and outputs and the extent to which output exceeds input. There are many problems involved in conducting an evaluation of this type in a corporation that produces a product. The problems are multiplied in school systems since no product is involved and there is not always unanimity on what should constitute outputs and how they should be measured. In some cases the ability to measure more intangible outputs is lacking and therefore more readily measurable factors are commonly employed, such as achievement-test scores. In other cases, where it is recognized that longitudinal studies of graduates are needed, costs and the ability of school systems to successfully conduct such studies impose severe limitations.

It would be mistaken, however, to consider evaluation as limited to the terminal stage of the policy process. Actually, evaluation occurs in some form at each stage of the policy-development process; if this were not so, unwise decisions could not be rescinded at any particular point in the process. Evaluation is the first step in improving policy.

After the findings are interpreted, the policy-maker must determine their significance and how they will be used to change the policy process. The improvement of the policy process will be examined in greater detail in Chapter 5.

CHAPTER 3

The Sources of Policy

POSSIBLE SOURCES OF POLICY

One of the most basic problems faced by the policy-maker is knowing the sources from which policy can be drawn. The policy-maker does not wish to be accused of being arbitrary, capricious, or Machiavellian; he prefers to be considered fair and equitable. Apart from action taken in the dissemination and implementation of policy, the reasonableness of the policy-maker is enhanced by his having a substantive basis for the development of policy. There are many possible sources of policy; among the more salient ones are philosophy, science, value systems, educational aims, educational standards, public opinion, and futuristic studies. The possibilities of each as a source of a systematic set of institutional policies will be examined in turn.

PHILOSOPHY

"All philosophy," says Alfred North Whitehead, "is an endeavor to obtain a self-consistent understanding of things observed."[1] Since the ancient Greeks often equated philosophy and rational thought, they thought of philosophy as the rational explanation of anything. Later, philosophy was considered to be the study of the first principles of being —human knowledge of ultimate reality. With the rise of modern science and the emergence of new disciplines, many of which are completely separate from philosophy, the role of philosophy, at least as defined in a more restricted sense by analytic philosophers, is limited to the study of meaning and verification or as the analysis of language and concepts. Not all philosophers today, however, would accept these interpretations and limitations; various idealists, existentialists, phenomenologists, and others would demur. For our purposes, we will consider philosophy, then, in the original meaning.

Policy, from this point of view, should not be isolated but part of a larger, more systematic whole. Philosophy provides a systematic, coherent framework within which policy can be embraced. Policy also needs an underlying rationale, and philosophy can supply it. A sense of purpose and direction is also sorely needed, and philosophy is sought for its ability to provide these things. Thus philosophy is generally considered one of the most valuable sources of policy.

There are some fundamental objections which could be raised, however. John S. Brubacher presents two shortcomings of this approach: first, there is no one-to-one correspondence between a philosophy and a set of policies; and second, there may be considerable overlap of philosophies in support of a policy.[2]

One reason why no one-to-one correspondence exists between philosophy and policy is that philosophy is not a deductive system like geometry. Thus it is not possible to strictly deduce from a general philosophy a set of educational policies or practices. Since, according to Philip G. Smith, philosophies are not "isomorphic systems presenting differing answers to a common set of questions," it would be more accurate to identify philosophies in terms of the types of questions they emphasize and the different ways they formulate basic problems.[3]

By examining educational history it can be seen that a variety of educational policies have been derived from philosophies. Idealism as a philosophical and metaphysical base has generated a number of different policies and practices. These policies have ranged from moderate to libertarian in the hands of such prominent idealists as Friedrich Froebel and Herman H. Horne to the fascistic policies espoused by the Italian idealist and educator Giovanni Gentile. Moreover, the philosopher's policy proposals are likely to be affected by new knowledge from educational research, advances in the social and behavioral sciences, and changing social and cultural conditions, even though the metaphysical base of his philosophy—the base from which, presumably, policy allegedly could be drawn—remains essentially unaltered. This is illustrated by Smith in his presentation of the proposals for educational policy and practice of three generations of idealists.[4] Moving chronologically from William T. Harris to Herman H. Horne to J. Donald Butler, it is possible to see a transition in their advocacy of desirable classroom-management procedures from control and obedience to greater permissiveness.

Secondly, there is considerable overlap among philosophies in their support of educational policy. Idealists, realists, and pragmatists, for instance, have usually supported democratic policies. While differences can be found among them in matters of interpretation and advocacy, these differences may not necessarily stem as much from metaphysical disagreements as from differences in educational aims. Moreover, differences can also be found in policy matters among those of the same philosophical position.

In light of the problems in utilizing a philosophical system as a basis for deriving policy, one may be inclined to consider philosophy a fruitless source of policy. This is not the case, however. Actually, a number of philosophical assumptions underlie any institution's policy network, and these certainly merit examination. Such notions about policy as continuity, temporality, predictability, permanence and change, order, and others are always present if one looks deeper than surface features. Policies need a sense of continuity within a time sequence; they always take place within a temporal framework and gain their meaning, at least in part, from this framework. Policies are also designed to bring about predictable changes in organizations, and policies that are conspicuously lacking in predictability, whatever their other merits, are usually not considered to be very good policies. It is also the case that organizations need a certain minimal sense of order derived from their policy operations in order to maintain continuity, to avoid unnecessary confusion and misplaced effort, and to achieve their goals more efficiently. In this sense, both permanence and change are sought. Although it would be misleading to speak of organizational permanence in an absolute sense, every organization is concerned with maintaining a sense of permanence and order within a given time spectrum while attempting to bring about controlled changes whenever existing policies fail to realize goals.

In conclusion, although philosophies cannot be utilized for deriving policies, there are a host of philosophical issues and assumptions which merit careful consideration by policy-makers; otherwise deliberations on policy are likely to be superficial, unsystematic, and possibly have untoward results.

THEORY

The possible connection between theory and practice has been investigated by a number of educators. It may prove instructive to examine the problem of moving from theory to practice because this problem is roughly analogous to that of moving from theory to policy.

Dewey notes that when theories and principles are comprehended it enables the teacher to move away from blind rule-following and act on the basis of an understanding of behavior.[5] In other words, the value of theory "resides in the enlightenment and guidance it supplies to observation and judgments of actual situations as they arise."[6] The main function of theory for Dewey is to move teachers away from the slavish following of rules so that their range of observation and understanding is broadened and a wider range of experiences, filled with greater meaning, can be drawn upon.

Just as in the case of philosophy and practice, some educational philosophers reject the belief that a logical connection exists between theory and practice. In repudiating such a connection, Thomas J. Howell raises the question whether any controls are exercised over education by philosophical beliefs.[7] Using a military analogy, he holds that the "strategies" and "grand designs" found in educational activities and organizations are influenced by philosophical beliefs. He attempts to show by illustrations that this does occur, even though no strict logical relations between the two activities exist.

Other educators, while agreeing that no strict logical relations exist between theory and practice, disagree as to the exact nature of the relationship, if any. D. Bob Gowin, for instance, holds that the function of educational theory is to guide practice and that a guide to practice contains "conditional oughts" which take the form, "In case of fire, break glass, and remove fire extinguisher."[8] Scientific theories and educational theories differ, he claims, insofar as the former deal with things to be manipulated while the latter refer to the person to be educated. Since education concerns itself with persons, it must specify the nature of moral responsibility entailed in the theory.

Certain objections can be raised against this interpretation. Henry J. Perkinson, for instance, rejects the argument that we should elucidate the moral responsibility entailed by the theory and offers in its stead the alternative of abandoning the term *educational theory* for *educational strategy*.[9] Strategies take the form: Under conditions *C*, do *Y*, if you want results *R*. The educational strategist does not concern himself with the moral dimension, whereas the educational practitioner, the person who uses the strategies, is concerned about the moral value certain strategies will bring about. The success of strategies, Perkinson believes, is accounted for by theories which focus on describing what is the case; yet we do not need to wait until theories are corroborated before developing strategies.

Some would object to the use of strategies on the grounds that they limit educational research to means and neglect the moral dimension among those who develop educational strategies. The critical problem, as Gowin sees it, is to show how one can engage in educational theorizing without, on the one hand, becoming an educational reformer through the tendency to overemphasize the moral dimension and, on the other hand, becoming a narrow educational scientist due to an inclination to deemphasize the moral dimension.[10]

Finally, George Newsome holds that although what is theoretically possible may not be practically feasible, and practitioners themselves must rely upon their own judgments, theory can provide more reliable and systematic understanding of education among practitioners even though no necessary connection exists between theory and practice.[11]

Thus some observers agree that the attempt to claim a logical connection between theory and practice is untenable; however, subsequent attempts to develop a defensible position that would enlist the support of leaders in the field have failed to achieve widespread agreement.

In terms of policy, although there is no strict logical connection between theory and policy, theory, nonetheless, has a function to play in the policy process. Descriptive theory (as opposed to normative theory) provides models to be used as a framework for explaining the operations of the policy process. Values and goals, which policy attempts to fulfill, are not derived from descriptive theory. They are, however, embodied in normative theory.

One example of the way in which theory is used to explain the policy process is the use of general systems theory. In this case, policy is viewed as part of an organizational system which attempts to maintain certain predetermined relationships in both internal and external environments through the use of regulative mechanisms. Another theory used to explain the policy process is decision-making theory, which, as seen earlier, has certain fundamental limitations in its applicability to the policy process. Thus, although no logically necessary relations exist between theory and policy, theoretical systems can be employed for their explanatory power in elucidating the dynamics and relationships of the policy-making process within organizations.

SCIENCE

If we include the social and behavioral sciences as well as the physical and biological sciences, it would appear at first glance that a vast range of possibilities is open to the policy-maker. The sciences, because of their status and their ability to corroborate knowledge claims, are usually considered one of the primary sources for the development of policy.

There are a number of ways that various sciences and a scientific approach to policy-making can be employed. Scientific surveys can be made of existing policies, in order to evaluate their outcomes and to determine how personnel and others affected react to them. Attitudes, incentives, and motivation of personnel are important factors in the operation of organizations, and policy-makers are usually concerned that these factors be adequately considered in any decisions that may lead to the modification of existing policy or the development of new policy.

In addition to the above uses of policy, are there more direct ways by which policy can be derived from science? Of course, one or more variants of the scientific method can be used in surveying and evaluating the policy operation, which is an important function; nonetheless, the basis for using science or scientific findings as a source of policy is less clear. One approach would be to conduct studies of organizations that seem to have optimized their outcomes and achieved results that are worth emulating. In such cases, the policies and operations of one organization become a model for another, and if it is assumed that the characteristics and goals of the two organizations are not overly dissimilar, this is certainly not an unreasonable approach to employ. One might still question whether the policy-makers in the organization to be emulated originally used science as a source for policy.

Keeping in mind the basic normative features of policy presented earlier, it would be misleading to contend that policy can be derived exclusively from a scientific base. At best, scientific findings would be combined in various relationships with other factors. Whatever these other factors in any given case, the very nature of policy would require that they be normative ingredients. Moreover, since science is not essentially prescriptive, while policy is prescriptive, it would be unlikely, for this reason, that a set of policies could be derived from science alone. However, the combination of scientific findings and various normative statements might very well be used as a source of policy. An example of this would be in school systems that have explicitly stated a set of humanistic goals; they should expect their operations not to conflict with or contradict those goals but be consistent with and facilitate them. For instance, a school system may express the goal of teaching students to respect the dignity and worth of each individual and to honor and safeguard his constitutionally protected rights. At the same time, if the policies of the school, whether deliberate or unintentional, create unequal opportunities and segregated learning environments, these policies would be inconsistent with professed goals.

Returning to humanistic educational goals, a set of policies should be informed by authoritative findings about man or "human nature." Knowledge would be needed about human characteristics, cultural uniformities and diversities, human potentialities, the effects of various learning environments, and similar matters. The normative dimension is introduced in determining within this range of social and behavioral findings what characteristics are most worthy of emphasis, which ones should be prized and preserved, which others should be discouraged or eliminated. For instance, after the policy-maker examines the findings, he may discover that both altruistic and aggressive features were found among the many characteristics. He may, for example, choose to emphasize the former and attempt to eliminate or discourage the latter. Science, in this case, has provided him with reliable knowledge. He brings to bear his value system or the value system prized by the school in determining which norms should take precedence in the determination of policy. The justification for the use of one set of values rather than another is another matter, however. This problem will be examined later in greater detail. At this point, however, it is important to remember that science does have a significant place in the policy process, not only in terms of assessing organizational characteristics and evaluating outcomes but also in providing policy-makers with reliable findings to inform their normative decisions.

VALUE SYSTEMS

Since policy is essentially normative in character, it would seem only logical that value systems constitute a prime source for policy development. However, it is necessary to be specific about the covering term *value systems*. For purposes of analysis, the study of values can be divided into moral, aesthetic, and utility values. By briefly delineating each in turn we will be in a better position to determine in what way, if any, each may serve as a source for policy.

The study of moral values has three divisions: empirical studies; normative ethics; and metaethics. Empirical studies are conducted to determine the moral beliefs of a population, the discrepancies between professed beliefs and actual practices, intercultural differences in moral values, the relationship of morality to law and customs in a particular society, the development of moral concepts in the child, and other matters. Normative ethics is concerned with right conduct. It propounds a system of ethics by which men should live, such as Stoicism, Epicureanism, Kantian ethics, utilitarianism, and others. Metaethics, on the other hand, deals with the meaning of ethical terms and how these terms are used in everyday discourse; it also seeks to distinguish moral from nonmoral terms, to determine how ethical judgments can be justified, and to inquire into the logic of moral reasoning.

Aesthetic values pertain to art, art objects, and standards of beauty; they deal with standards of taste and judgment in art, and develop theories about these matters. Aesthetics is also concerned with the process of experiencing art and the qualities and characteristics of aesthetic experience. Aesthetics, in contrast to some of the other areas of philosophy, now includes detailed empirical studies as well as normative theories.

Utility values relate to the comparative worth, value, or usefulness of a process, operation, or product within a particular social context. The appraisal of the worth of competing products for home, business, or industry is one type of study in this area. Also, the appraisal of the value of certain types of institutional operations, which may or may not involve the use and manipulation of products, is another type of study. Decision-making theory, as it was discussed earlier, would also be part of this area of inquiry.

Whether or not a formal value system is adopted, value assumptions relating to various value positions are evident in educational programs. To the extent that these values tend to determine the structure and direction of programs, the policies which are then adopted to regulate and provide guidelines for programs are thereby influenced by these values. Thus the policies serve the values rather than the other way around. As discussed earlier, policy is normative in character and is context-dependent; whereas the values are more independent of context and take the form of general norms, which may serve as basic value assumptions (when no systematic value system is used) or educational aims. Policies, then, establish operating procedures used to fulfill the adopted values. Thus the policy-maker may often have a role in the determination of school values or the values assumptions underlying some aspect of education, such as the curriculum. He must also see that proposed policies are reasonably consistent with basic values and that the policies adopted will best fulfill them. At the same time, since efficacy is not the sole criterion for determining the appropriateness of chosen policies, it will be necessary to appraise side-effects in order to make certain that they do not undermine another set of accepted values.

Policy would fall within the category of utility values. Values of this type, in contrast to moral and aesthetic values, are essentially utilitarian. But policy is not so much a utility value as a utility process, which receives its sense of direction and purpose from utility, moral, or aesthetic values. Policy operations may also have moral consequences, and policy decisions may affect aesthetic values. Thus, there are many interconnecting links between policy and these three types of values.

CHAPTER 4

Policy Operations in Their Organizational Setting

POLICY NETWORKS

Policy operations and processes are characteristically found in an organizational or an institutional setting. Among the features that organizations share is the use of policy to regulate operations and establish innovational alternatives to existing programs. The stability of organizational processes and the capacity to undertake new functions are determined to a considerable degree by the quality and types of policy which they develop.

Organizations have proliferated in today's society, organizations of divergent size, structure, and purposes to serve public and private interests. There are educational, industrial, governmental, labor, recreational, medical, legal, and other organizations. The growth of large-scale organizations has been a characteristic feature of industrial societies during this century. These would include the large bureaus and subdivisions of government and labor, the growth of what Clark Kerr calls the "multiversity," and the largest metropolitan school districts. Designed to perform large-scale tasks more efficiently, these organizations have come under severe criticism in recent years. The criticisms range from charges of waste and inefficiency to accusations that the organizations dehumanize the very persons they are designed to serve.

Policy networks are characteristic features of all but the smallest and youngest organizations. In order for an organization to grow and develop and fulfill its goals, those responsible for policy decisions initiate a continuous process of formulating, disseminating, implementing, and evaluating policy. Over a period of time an organization develops policies governing its most important operations.[1] At this stage of development an organization can also be said to have an official position on important policy matters; and although some policies may be tacitly understood, the most vital policies affecting the organization's basic operations and its immediate future will be formulated. These policies,

43

although diverse and pertaining to many different facets of the organization's operations, are related to one another in a policy network. In other words, they form a network by which an observer can gain a profile, an accurate depiction of the organization's overall operations. Policies are not usually related in a logical manner in the sense of being logically deducible from one another. A strict logical relation would only obtain if policy-makers used a rationalistic model consisting of basic axioms and postulates or universal principles from which subsidiary principles could be derived to govern policy choice. There is evidence that the development of policy does not proceed in this manner.[2] Thus we can speak of policy networks as providing a profile of an organization's operations, but these networks are unlikely to be understood by applying a rationalistic model.

Policy networks are better explained and understood through the use of a functional model. Functional models use purposive explanations. In explanations of this type, the given or discovered meanings are part of the constituent explanations for the resultant actions. The acts are considered to be purposive, although, as with children playing games, the purpose may not lie outside the acts themselves. Functional models examine activities in terms of purposes served in a culture by the activity, rather than searching for the motives of the participants. Since there are unanticipated and unintended consequences of actions, not all acts serve a function in a culture. Moreover, some activities which once served a function no longer do so. Through historical studies their original function can be uncovered; other studies would be needed, however, to ascertain their current persistence in face of the disappearance of function. Of course it could be claimed that they are still functional since otherwise they would not persist; but this would be to assume that all acts have a function (which would be exceedingly difficult to support) and it would also ignore the dysfunctional, as well as nonfunctional, features of certain acts.

One way by which an organization's operations can be understood is by analyzing its policy network, which can best be accomplished by employing a functional model to see the functions served by the respective policies and how these functions relate to one another. This approach also provides a perspective on the relation of the policy network to organizational goals by noting how the various functions in concert help to support and fulfill these goals.

This can be seen more readily in the operations of school systems. A great many policies are established by local school boards; others originate at the state or federal level in terms of regulations surrounding funding and programs. Whatever leeway remains in policy-making is given over to principals and, occasionally, to teachers. Of course the relative proportion of policy originating at each of the respective levels varies from one region, state, or school district to another. As we look at policies regulating finance, buildings and facilities, curricula, interpersonal relations, and a host of other aspects of a school system, an examination can be made of the functions which these policies serve. In such an investigation it is important to look for the interrelationship of functions—how they complement, reinforce, or obstruct one another —in order to discern their total configuration in relationship to the system's goals. Through use of this approach, meaningful relationships can be perceived and evaluations can be conducted, enabling the observer to determine the extent to which the policy outcomes contribute to or inhibit the system's attaining of its goals. Additionally, the relationship between means and objectives can be more critically assessed by determining consistency between policies and goals. Assume, for instance, that the system has established progressive goals (i.e., some of those originated in the progressive movement), policies regulating teacher-pupil interaction, classroom and extraclass activities, should not establish practices which are more in keeping with traditional forms of education. Policies may be established, even though the goals are otherwise, that are sufficiently restrictive that teachers must scrupulously employ a lecture-recitation approach and rely almost exclusively on assigned texts. Thus, giving attention to the functions served by policies can highlight discrepancies between means and ends.

BUREAUCRACY IN EDUCATION

Bureaucratic systems are not unique features of our time; they can be found in the Roman Empire and in other early civilizations. Moreover, even in American education bureaucratic school systems developed as early as 1875 and spread widely by the turn of the century.[3] What is distinctive about our own age in this regard is the extent to which bureaucratic systems have spread through government, business, labor, education, and other areas of the culture.

Bureaucracy has become a pejorative term today, but it was originally conceived in a more neutral or descriptive sense. Max Weber developed a model of the formal operations of bureaucracies.[4] The objectives of bureaucracy are to elevate speed, precision, and continuity, heighten rationality in operations, reduce friction, and minimize costs. Bureaucracies, in other words, operate on the principle of efficiency, and they are designed to be more efficient than organizations that base their operations on other models.

There are several ways that efficiency can be maximized through the arrangement of organizational structures and processes. A hierarchical system of offices is employed in which each office is controlled and supervised by a higher one. Qualifications for positions are stated in writing, and employment is based on hiring the person best qualified to fulfill the position. Thus, theoretically speaking, bureaucracies are removed from political patronage. The functions of each office are specified by a set of written rules delineating the scope of responsibility for each office-holder. Qualifications for employment are based on specialized abilities and skills; the route to advancement is determined by achievement and seniority. By employing the most qualified people, heightening rationality, providing attractive features of promotion and protection against arbitrary dismissal, and utilizing consistent and uniform rules that standardize performance of tasks, the bureaucratic model is supposed to increase effectiveness in the application of technical and experimental knowledge and thereby maximize efficiency.

Following this ideal type or model it would only be reasonable to expect bureaucratic organizations to be more efficient than nonbureaucratic systems, which are likely to be less systematically organized. But numerous complaints are commonly heard today that seriously call into question the adequacy of bureaucracies to perform their appointed tasks.

A common criticism is that bureaucracies, rather than being more efficient than other types of organizations, are actually more inefficient, self-serving, cluttered with "red tape," and run by curt time-servers. It is well known that such charges are true in the case of a number of bureaucracies. The question arises why bureaucracies have so often failed to achieve their own standards—much less the standards that others expect of them? The obvious answer, for those who believe in the bureaucratic model, is that they have failed in some way to conduct their operations according to the model. In other words, qualified observers would be able to uncover defective practices in staffing, promotion, retention, communication to subordinates, or some other area.

A more impressive literature is available to show that management or administration has frequently neglected to consider carefully the effects of informal relationships in the system—the types of group work patterns and influences that are not to be found on organizational charts.[5] Informal groups arise spontaneously in work situations to fulfill a social need not met through the formal structure. Productivity, qual-

ity of work, job satisfaction, and morale may all be influenced significantly by informal groups. Thus the failure of management and
supervisory personnel to understand and relate effectively to the informal group structure of an organization is one possible source of failure.

There may be considerably more interaction among workers in
some industries than among teachers. Despite changes made by some
schools, teaching, in the self-contained classroom, remains a semipri-
vate affair. There are, to be sure, periodic classroom visits by the principal and supervisors; still, observations of teaching practices are far more
common during the probationary period than among tenured faculty.
Teachers rarely visit one another's classes. "In most schools teachers
practice their own methods—rarely hearing, or even caring, if one of
their colleagues is experimenting with some new teaching device or
technique."[6] Thus the findings from industry on informal group influence seem to be less applicable to teachers.

Teachers are concerned, just as is the case with semiprofessionals
and professionals in other areas of public service, with the seemingly
geometric progression of paperwork and endless forms, the multiplica-
tion of nonteaching duties, and the ostensible unresponsiveness of the
administration to teachers' interests. The cause of these problems may
be attributed to such factors as unconcern, incompetence, inadequate
planning, poor policies, and a rigid bureaucracy.

In recent years, students have charged bureaucratic school systems
and universities with being a principal source of growth of feelings of
alienation and dehumanization. They contend that such systems are so
large and impersonal that students are no longer treated as persons but
as things, numbers on an IBM card, faceless entities, more like robots
than humans. One reason for the breakdown in bureaucracies is the
sheer size and complexity of operations, which render the processes far
too unwieldy to be handled effectively. This would call for new, smaller
decentralized systems.

A criticism of a different, more penetrating type holds that alienation, while exacerbated by size and complexity, is due to ideological
conflict. The guiding ideology of administration, some students contend, is some form of conservative or liberal doctrine which is no longer
adequate to cope with the massive problems—educational and otherwise—of our time. Thus a minority of students, through various forms
of protest, civil disobedience, and occasionally violence, seek to bring
about structural changes that are undergirded by a new ideology and
new set of aims.

It could well be true that many conflicts arise as much from ideological differences as from the structure of bureaucracy. However, certain

theoretical assumptions, which underlie the structure, may very well conflict with the values of some students. We could hypothesize that organizational structure imposes a set of constraints on policy. We need to raise, then, the following question: How and to what extent are educational policies influenced by organizational structure? In responding to the question, it will be necessary to present some related features of bureaucracies and their operations.

THE INFLUENCES OF BUREAUCRACY ON POLICY

Many general characteristics and functions of bureaucratic organizations apply to any type of bureaucracy—education, business, labor, or government. On the other hand, researchers have used various classificatory schemes in order to delineate different types of organizations. Alfred Kuhn, for instance, using allocation of costs and values as distinguishing criteria, lists four types of organizations: cooperative, profit, service, and pressure organizations.[7]

The cooperative organization produces for itself, pays its own costs, and is the recipient of the benefits. Examples are trade and professional organizations that provide services for their members; consumer and productive cooperatives; social, fraternal, sports, and hobby organizations; legitimate government (when it serves the interests of the people); and church congregations (insofar as they serve their members rather than performing missionary or charitable work).[8]

Profit organizations are the second type. The costs of operation are borne by recipients who buy the goods or pay for the services. The objective of the organization is aggrandizement: to make profits on goods sold and services rendered. Although private businesses and corporations are typical of this type of organization, rackets and other criminal groups, churches, schools, charities, and fraternal organizations that have been converted into profit operations are also included in this classification.

Service organizations, the third type, are distinguished by the fact that sponsors bear the costs and the benefits go to the recipients as gifts. Charities, subsidized education, charitable and missionary activities of churches, nonprofit research firms, and groups organized to protect civil liberties, provide emergency services, and offer free legal aid are all organizations of this type.

Finally, pressure organizations direct their activities toward recipients who neither shoulder the costs nor receive the benefits. The objective of these organizations is to influence the recipients in such a manner that power relations will be changed to benefit the sponsors. Examples are labor unions, trade associations (that are not cooperatives), lobbies, political parties, and propaganda agencies.

Educational systems, in terms of the above classification scheme, would be considered service organizations. There are, of course, numerous other possibilities in classifying organizations. The scheme could be based on specifying the prime beneficiaries of the system. For instance, Blau and Scott delineate four types of organizations on the basis of this criterion:[9]

TYPE	BENEFICIARY
Mutual Benefit Associations	Membership
Business Concerns	Owners
Service Organizations	Client Group
Commonwealth Associations	Public-at-Large

In the above schema, school systems, in terms of beneficiaries, exhibit features of both service organizations and commonwealth associations. Other criteria, however, might also be employed: for example, size, public or private, centralized or decentralized, membership, function performed in the larger society. But it is not necessary to multiply classificatory schemes; our discussion so far should be sufficient to indicate the differences between various types of organizations and to identify educational systems among these different types. Now that these differences have been presented, we turn to certain features found in all bureaucracies while noting the specific form they take in educational organizations.

Authority

Max Weber speaks of "legitimate authority" based on "rational grounds," a type commonly found in bureaucracies.[10] This type of authority is based on a recognition of the legality of the patterns of normative rules and the right of those holding positions of authority to issue commands. In contrast, according to Weber, "power" is the probability that a person within a social relationship will be able to carry out his will despite resistance.[11] Bureaucratic officeholders seek to use legitimate authority but may also resort to the use of power when resistance is met in carrying out their policies. Since there is an implication of voluntary compliance to legal authority, in many cases it is difficult to know whether or not compliance is actually voluntary. Certainly in any organization there is, in addition to legal authority, the use of power, persuasion, work-group influences, and incentives in getting personnel to abide by organizational norms, execute policies, and fulfill standards.

The administrator who holds office can be spoken of as holding de jure authority;[12] that is, he gains his authority by the legitimacy accorded the normative rules and his recognized right to enforce them. This type of authority would differ from the authority of the expert or of the charismatic leader. Occasionally an administrator's policies are followed because teachers recognize his expertise in a particular policy area; less frequently, officials exhibit charismatic qualities that encourage others to follow them. But most officials, however, rely on the authority of their office in exercising social control and enforcing policies. Nevertheless, even if the official is not charismatic, it is not uncommon for him to employ human-relations skills and techniques of persuasion. Teachers usually expect their principal to relate successfully to the faculty and students by showing a sensitive awareness of their needs and problems.

Once personnel accept the legitimacy of the normative rules and the right of the officeholder to enforce them, they cannot ask whether the rule is moral or right or should be obeyed. They can legitimately inquire whether the officeholder has interpreted or applied the rule correctly. Nonetheless, it can be argued that personnel, while accepting the legitimacy of an administrator's legal authority, might question whether a set of policies, old or new, are inconsistent or in conflict with the goals the organization is designed to serve. The very fact that the official holds office gives him the powers vested in that office and ascribes legal authority to him. It does not, however, make him "an authority" automatically in the sense of possessing a special expertise in policy matters (although it would be foolish for a school board to appoint him to the position if he lacked expertise in policy matters). Since it is not unknown for officeholders to lack certain requisite abilities, one can evaluate how well they perform the duties of the office. Once again, evaluation depends on the system's rules, which prescribe who is responsible for conducting the evaluation—and, in a number of school systems, teachers are not expected to participate in such evaluations. Additionally, even if the official is an expert, experts make mistakes, sometimes display tunnel-vision, and therefore need to be evaluated.

The structural framework for authority in bureaucracies is hierarchical. In school systems the school board exercises authority in formulating the basic policies that regulate the system. These policies relate to curriculum, personnel practices, regulations governing students, finance, and buildings and materials. Most school boards maintain jurisdiction over the latter two areas while, in some cases, delegating authority to the superintendent and his associates to set policies in the other areas, subject to the board's approval. The range of a board's activities, of course, varies from one district to another, but the board is vested with the legal authority to decide all basic policy matters except those state education policies that take precedence over local policies and federal-aid policies attached to particular programs in the local district. The state can pass laws that countermand existing policies and practices, as in the case of the Massachusetts Racial Imbalance Law, whose application in the case of Boston schools threatened a loss of state aid unless local policy was changed to comply with the law.[13] And there have also been numerous pressures by the U.S. Office of Education to get local school districts, especially in the South, to comply with federal desegregation guidelines.

As a school district's operations enlarge by an expansion in programs and the hiring of new personnel to staff these programs, the hierarchical system also enlarges and grows more complex in order to administer and supervise new programs and personnel. Whenever growth of this type occurs, it increases the likelihood of a breakdown in the dissemination of new policies from the central administration. This breakdown is more likely in schools where the student population has grown rapidly, as in the case where a new, large industry opens in a community, resulting in an influx of new families; or, in other instances, where an older school system has become increasingly unwieldy and the administration no longer is able to successfully cope with changes.

In his study of the New York City school system, David Rogers found a number of hierarchical problems that lead to a breakdown in communication among the various units.[14] He found the system to be overcentralized, with many levels in the chain of command. This condition was coupled with vertical and horizontal fragmentation that isolated units from one another and limited communication and coordination of functions. It was also found that the administration and the board were insulated from clients; thus, not only was there a breakdown in communication, but the system became more unresponsive to the needs of various publics.

In such cases, where communication between the administration and personnel in the system's subunits is impaired, the inability to disseminate policy statements as intended leads to an incapacity to execute policy properly. Thus, various proposals have been made for streamlining bureaucratic systems; others have opted for the decentralization of large metropolitan schools, leading thereby to varying degrees of community control.

Another problem facing such systems is the inability of the administration to get personnel to voluntarily comply with school policies (assuming, in this instance, that no serious problem in communication exists). There are a number of ways by which the administration maintains control over the system and ensures that its policies are properly implemented. Most prominent among these is the concept of "legal authority"; other approaches include the use of power, persuasion, work-group influences, and human-relations skills. Another characteristic feature of organizations is their use of sanctions (rewards and punishments) to gain the compliance of personnel. Rewards may consist of monetary inducements, honors, or words of praise and appreciation; sanctions include verbal rebukes, salary freezes, lack of promotion, heavier teaching loads, less desirable teaching schedules, and, finally, dismissal. Sanctions of these various types can be debated on pragmatic grounds in terms of their ability to achieve desired results; or they may be criticized as being inhumane or, perhaps, inappropriate ways of handling professionals. Nonetheless, the members of the administration can invoke the legal authority vested in their office as the source of legitimacy. When these tactics fail, the question can be raised whether the administration has the power to bring about intended behaviors when such behaviors are no longer voluntarily undertaken. An overt show of power, however, is usually avoided except under those conditions—such as work stoppages, student violence, etc.—where other procedures have failed. There are, of course, notorious exceptions where an administration acts precipitously prior to exploring rational exchanges of ideas and the use of persuasion. Power, for the most part, is veiled; it is present but latent; it differs from the policeman's power, which is displayed more openly. But the very fact that the administration must resort to the use of power may prove self-defeating even if it brings about a recognition among recalcitrant personnel that they lack power to effect a redress of grievances. Most often the use of power, especially when frequently invoked prior to utilizing negotiation and other procedures, will lead to lowered morale and furtive disobedience.

It would be mistaken, however, to believe that all administrations seek to maintain control and system equilibrium at the cost of other values. Though there are numerous administrations, both in urban and rural areas, that strive to do this very thing, there are notable examples of new superintendents who were brought in by a board for the purpose of initiating widespread innovations and reorganizing the bureaucratic machinery.[15] Admittedly, however, there is a pronounced tendency in many organizations, especially school systems, to strive to maintain order and equilibrium at all costs, even though it is likely to stifle creativity and fruitful innovation. Moreover, to employ the equilibrium model is to blind oneself to the deeper questions about the desirability of the organization's goals and its internal operating relationships.

The deficiencies of the equilibrium model will be examined later; at this point it may be advisable to qualify some of the early observations about social control. Amitai Etizoni classifies organization in terms of the type of control or authority used.[16] The types of authority are coercive, utilitarian, normative, and mixed. Coercive authority is found in prisons, concentration camps, prisoner-of-war camps, custodial mental institutions, and some unions. Utilitarian authority, based on economic incentives, is characteristic of business and industry, business unions, farmers' organizations, and peacetime military organizations. Normative authority, based on status, membership, and intrinsic value rewards, is found in hospitals, religious organizations, ideologically based political organizations, social unions, and voluntary and professional organizations. Finally, mixed forms of authority are found in most labor unions (utilitarian-normative), combat units (normative-coercive), and some early industries, company towns, farms, and ships (utilitarian-coercive).

Historically speaking, the forms of educational authority—or, more accurately, "control"—have been mixed. The coercive form has been limited (except as applied to students); but utilitarian controls have been used even though monetary rewards and promotions could not act as powerful incentives. The attractiveness of tenure to many teachers, and its appeal to their need for security, served for many years as a powerful utilitarian means of control. Teachers seek to abide by administrative policies in exchange for assurance of security in their jobs. With the rise of teachers' unions and the growing use of collective bargaining, strikes, and sanctions, utilitarian controls are cast in a new light. When the issues revolve around working conditions, salaries, and fringe benefits, teachers become more concerned with unions or teacher organizations that can secure them benefits and thereby weaken the utilitarian controls used by administrators; on the other hand, it shifts the focus of concern away from normative controls.

Normative controls, based on status, membership, and intrinsic rewards, and where the emphasis is placed more on service to society than on personal gain, are the appropriate form of control for school systems because teachers, first of all, are primarily engaged in the performance of a public service and, secondly, because professions and semiprofessions chiefly utilize normative controls. It could, of course, be argued that teaching has yet to establish itself as a profession and it would therefore be inappropriate for administrators to use normative controls exclusively. True, teaching may not measure up to law, medicine, and engineering in terms of certain professional criteria; but, once again, the extent to which an occupational group fulfills professional criteria is always a matter of degree. Teachers range from semiprofessional to professional; teaching should probably be referred to as an "emerging profession." Teachers who have little opportunity to utilize their full range of ability and to continue to grow as professional persons because of the bureaucratic structure and the types of controls to which they are subject, are unlikely to develop their professional qualities. Thus normative controls should be chief form used in school systems.

Size and Centralization

The rise of metropolitan areas early in this century, the growth of suburban areas more recently, and the continual consolidation of school districts have brought about an appreciable growth in the size of school systems. Among 18,600 school districts in the United States in 1969, 21.5 million students out of a total 45.5 million attended school systems with an enrollment size of 10,000 or more.[17] New York City's schools educate more students than the states of Delaware, Montana, Nevada, New Hampshire, New Mexico, North Dakota, Rhode Island, Utah, and Vermont combined. Clearly, size itself is one of the principal ingredients in bureaucratic school systems.

Along with size, school systems have become increasingly centralized as the complex growth of functions and services has accelerated. As systems become more centralized, structural arrangements become less functional for delegating authority, which, in turn, tends to render policy-making an operation from the top down rather than involving participation at the middle and lower rungs of the ladder.

It is not an inevitable fact of organizational development that the greater the size, the more centralized the system becomes. General Motors, for instance, is so decentralized that various units are competitive and almost autonomous. According to Ernest Dale, there are certain advantages and disadvantages in decentralizing and shifting policy-making to lower management levels. Among the advantages: the people most concerned will be making the decisions and may be able to make better and faster decisions; a reduction of expense in central coordination; and an opportunity for the rank and file to assume responsibility and make decisions. Among the disadvantages: lack of uniformity of decisions; probable failure to use the advice of specialists who would be available in a centralized organization; duplication of effort;

and the fact that it is difficult for administrators to accept decentralization.[18]

There are various indications of a growing centralization in American education. There has been a rapid consolidation of school districts —from about 130,000 districts in 1930 to about 18,600 in 1969. Educators urged consolidation to provide a larger tax base, reduce costs, and enable the schools to offer more comprehensive curriculums. Today one-fourth of the nation's school systems educate nearly 80 percent of the students. There has been a growth, during the past decade, of the authority and functions performed by state departments of education and the U.S. Office of Education. As the size of the student population increases, there has been a trend toward greater centralization of school functions, including curriculum planning. And as size and centralization increase, there is a growth in the number of administrative offices between the classroom teacher and the superintendent.

Problems of communication are accentuated by large size and centralization. The more formally organized the hierarchy, the less the upward flow of informal communications. One study of a governmental agency showed that subordinates consulted with one another rather than with their supervisor out of fear that the supervisor would think of them as indecisive or weak.[19] There is also a tendency for communications traveling down the hierarchy to be critical, and for those traveling up the hierarchy from subordinates to be commendatory. In a laboratory experiment with groups where status differences were present, Harold Kelley found that low-status members were more likely to communicate upwards about irrelevant matters and be unwilling to criticize high-status members.[20] For the administrative hierarchy to improve communication, it must recognize the informal group relations that exist and tie its communication of policy into these groups. A problem of social control will also probably arise whenever the informal group structure is bypassed. Informal group norms that support the administration's position are needed before compliance with policy will be predictable and widespread.

There is considerable cross-pressure in the superintendent's role since he has to gain the support of many conflicting groups (including informal groups) if he is to successfully execute policy. The principal, too, has the problem of exercising leadership and maintaining good morale and working conditions for his staff while attempting to fulfill policies from the central administration that sometimes conflict with these objectives. One aspect of social control for the principal is the amount of supervision of faculty. Too much supervision may destroy morale, initiative, and independence; but insufficient supervision with difficult tasks may lead to confusion, disorganization, and a loss of confidence. The principal's decision in these matters must be made in terms of the competence and experience of the teacher, the difficulty and complexity of the task, and the conviction that teachers must be afforded sufficient autonomy to grow professionally.

Specialization and Standardization

It is well known that the development of an industrial civilization has led to greater specialization and standardization in industry; this trend is also evident in government with the growth of bureaucratic systems. Schools manifest these trends in a somewhat different way. The elimination of most one-room schools and the establishment of more rigorous certification requirements have brought about greater specialization in teaching. New administrative specialties have developed in large urban systems, such as public-relations positions and specialties in research, finance, personnel, and other fields. Supportive-service positions have also emerged: guidance and counseling, school psychologists, school nurses, curriculum specialists, instructional supervisors, media specialists, computer and scheduling experts, and many more.

There are a great many evidences of standardization in education. Certification requirements are more standardized (and, although differences still exist from one state to another, there is some reciprocity in recognizing teaching certificates from other states). Teachers still rely heavily on textbooks and standardized curriculum guides, which provide the basic sources for curriculum.[21] Other standardized features are the academic-year calendar, standardized classrooms and furniture, standardized tests, units of course credits, age grading, and promotion policies. Of course the teacher's work is not as standardized as the assembly-line worker's, and teachers are not readily interchangeable. The actual conduct of instruction is the one area where teachers have some freedom to define for themselves their own teaching activities; yet many teachers still rely heavily on standardized materials and also attempt to routinize instruction.

The standardization of education was not completely accidental; nor should it be thought of as a malevolent plot to subvert teaching. The role of the states in certification arose in response to widespread irregularities and inconsistencies among school districts in the employment of teachers. State certification attempted to raise standards by establishing more uniform, enforceable requirements.

Similar reasons can be given for other standardized aspects of education. Textbooks, standardized tests, and curriculum guides were also designed to aid the teacher and enhance his abilities in instruction and evaluation. With the growth in the size and complexity of school districts, administrators found it necessary to adopt policies that would help standardize and regulate programs more effectively. That many of the standardized aspects of education are under attack for allegedly stultifying the student's growth by placing him in a lockstep system that rewards obedience and rule-following rather than creativity may be due both to an unimaginative and overly rigid application of standardized procedures and to instituting the wrong forms of standardization. In the former case, when all policy-making is conducted from the top down, untoward results may be quite common. In the latter case, policy-makers need to reexamine the operations that are standardized, determine their effects, and then make the changes needed to best promote the school's goals. The desire of businessmen to have the schools run on an industrial-efficiency model can stifle the effectiveness of teachers.[22] The standardization of operations and programs, while scarcely unavoidable, should be examined closely to make certain that the desire for administrative efficiency and convenience does not stifle learning and crush initiative and independence. Private schools that have been expressly established as alternatives to public schools are usually far less standardized than most public schools. (See Vernon H. Smith, *Alternative Schools: The Development of Options in Public Education* [Lincoln, Nebr.: Professional Educators Publications, 1974].) These alternative school systems should be scrutinized to determine how their operations are conducted and the effects of decreased standardization on curriculum and instruction.

CHANGING BUREAUCRATIC SCHOOL SYSTEMS

Theoretical Changes

Up to this point our presentation of bureaucracies has been primarily descriptive rather than normative and evaluative; at this point our stance will be a critical one.

Several theoretical models and sets of assumptions underlying bureaucratic organizations must first be changed before substantial progress can be made in bringing about new types of school systems equipped to meet the demands of our times. Four concepts prominent in bureaucratic systems, which need to be critically reassessed, are *homeostasis, adaptation, equilibrium,* and *social control.*

Homeostatic models, derived from biology and also used in psychology, underlie organizational thinking. Homeostasis is a relatively stable state of equilibrium, or a tendency toward such a state by the subsystems of an organism or the individuals who constitute a group. At the organismic level, the organism attempts to maintain an internal balance through the proper coordinate functioning of different subsystems—for instance, the digestive, respiratory, circulatory, and lympathic systems. When the balance is disturbed, physiological drives—such as hunger, thirst, rest, and sex—propel the organism to act to overcome the internal deficiency; later, deficiencies again arise and the cycle repeats itself.

At the group level, the individual must subordinate and control any of his desires that runs counter to the group in order that the group's continued existence will not be threatened; this outcome is further assured by the application of sanctions and various pressures to prevent deviance. The group's leader attempts to instill a conviction in the worthwhileness of the group's activities and purposes, and strives to achieve a normative consensus so that there will be harmony of action and purpose. The leader recognizes that in democratically conducted groups, unanimity cannot be expected on all the norms; therefore the objective is to achieve a consensus on the substantive and procedural norms. The working consensus enables the group to survive and carry on its activities; the consensus, according to this model, represents the democratic give-and-take of discussion and decision-making. When consensus is not forthcoming or is temporarily caused by disagreements over new issues and problems, the tendency toward a relative stable group relationship has broken down; this breakdown leads to search behavior in which one or more group members attempt to restore stability by developing a new working consensus.

The homeostatic model of man has a number of weaknesses. It assumes that certain tensions create drives to restore an equilibrium and that the process is repeated ad infinitum. Man becomes a tension-reduction mechanism. His chief motivation is to relieve tensions and restore a stable organismic environment. But the model overlooks the fact that humans are much more than tension-reduction mechanisms. Man is purposeful, goal-directed, can live by ideals, and has the capacity to deliberately postpone or ignore the reduction of tensions when pursuing goals.

The weaknesses of the consensus model can best be highlighted by looking first at other theoretical assumptions of bureaucracies. Closely related to the tension-reduction notion, but in this case applied to overall organizational operations, is the concept of adaptation. Organizational change is explained by reference to an organization's ability to adapt to new developments. Changes, however, produce "strains" and "tensions," which occasionally cause maladaptive responses, either in the total organization or in one or more of its subunits. Any number of factors may precipitate strains and tensions: the failure of school-bond issues, student demonstrations and protests, pressure-group attacks on schools, teacher strikes, and so forth. The school system, in light of such disturbances, is depicted by the adaptation model as attempting to cope with change by cushioning its impact so that tensions do not reverberate throughout the system and render its coping ability maladaptive. Strategies are devised to handle anticipated disturbances before they get out of hand. The strategies represent the coping mechanisms used to maintain the organization's adaptive capacity. The application of the model does not involve a resistance to all forces of change; rather, it seeks to counter or cushion change factors that would render the organization maladaptive.

The difficulty with the model is that adaptation has become axiomatic; it becomes the guiding, unquestioned value to which all other values are secondary. As a result, adaptation may be pursued at too great a cost. The cost of the supremacy of adaptation in the value scheme is to ignore the question whether the organization actually should be preserved. Furthermore, it tends to deflect attention away from an independent evaluation of organizational goals and policies. Thus an organization may have unjust or discriminatory policies and its goals may be undesirable and harmful, but such matters are not evaluated in the adaptive model. Survival is always the first order of business, later to be followed by an attempt to achieve optimum operating conditions. The adaptive model is suited to totalitarian organizations and institutions as well as to democratic ones. Finally, the model offers no way to evaluate change factors apart from their impact upon the adaptability of the organization.

An equilibrium model of some type is commonly used in the social sciences to explain social systems and organizations. Sociologists study the components and functional relations of social systems. By examining the various prescribed roles of a system's participants and the way in which the fulfillment of these roles enables the system to successfully carry out its functions, an equilibrium model for the system can be developed to show how the system can be optimally organized. Social disorganization is based on the equilibrium model; it occurs when a sufficient number of key members of the system fail to perform prescribed roles adequately, leading to disorganization because the system can no longer fulfill its functions.

This outlook takes the social system of a society as given, so that abnormality is ascribed to individuals who break the norms irrespective of how corrupt and unjust the system may be. The situation is not better in political science, where such central concepts as power, authority, and legitimacy are used descriptively rather than normatively. Legitimacy is established by opinion surveys and authority in terms of decision-making as well as surveys. These terms have no connection with rightness, justice, or other normative concepts. The focus is upon how the system is able to maintain itself by achieving a dynamic equilibrium through the use of authority and power. Thus many political studies raise no normative questions about their data or findings. Such studies fail to focus upon such broad humanistic concerns as the type of political arrangements which will alleviate human suffering and provide the kind of environment in which all men can best fulfill their needs and develop their potentials.

Many contemporary social scientists, particularly sociologists, have centered their attention on the maintenance of existing structures through the use of social control rather than on the dynamics of conflict in social systems.[23] Organizations, it is widely believed, need structures that enable them to adapt to their environment, mobilize their resources for continued functioning, and integrate their activities to avoid disequilibrium. To accomplish these tasks, various forms of sanctions and other social controls are instituted. The focus in organizational theory has been on the maintenance of functions through the application of social controls, while the reality of social conflicts has generally been neglected.[24] Moreover, the fact that social conflict has important social functions has usually been overlooked, not so much by early sociologists as by contemporary ones.

Social conflict is defined by Lewis Coser as "a struggle over values and claims to scarce status, power and resources in which the aims of the opponents are to neutralize, injure, or eliminate their rivals."[25] Conflict, in this sense, has been a characteristic feature of world history, not only in terms of the disproportionate time span in which war, between groups and nations, rather than peace has dominated human life but also in terms of the less violent conflicts that are regular features of social systems. The attempt to delimit the study of organizations by restricting inquiry within the framework of homeostatic mechanisms, adaptation, consensus, equilibrium, and social control has resulted in a distorted and unrealistic depiction of organizational processes. On the other hand, the use of social conflict as the basic explanatory principle of organizational life would also be unrealistic. Yet it is important that the neglect of social conflict be rectified by recognizing that conflicts are characteristic features of organizations, that not all conflicts are deleterious, and that important changes have come about as a result of conflicts—and some of these changes may not have been possible by consensus techniques or other traditional forms of organizational operations. The latter contention, of course, is always open to debate due to different interpretations of data and the divergence of value systems found among individuals making the judgment. Nonetheless, it can plausibly be argued that America's independence from England was facilitated by the Revolutionary War; that the conflict over slavery could not be definitively settled short of war; that after 1939, the only way to stop Hitler from achieving his objectives was by going to war. It is also the case that the rapid advances of American labor during this century probably could not have been achieved without social conflict. In spite of beliefs that the Congress operates on a consensus model, conflict (as defined by Coser) is an important part of the legislative process. In education, the dramatic changes in the past few years in the National Education Association would have taken decades—assuming they would ever have occurred—if it had not been for that body's conflicts with the American Federation of Teachers. The use of teacher strikes and sanctions is another example of conflict—in many cases preceded by the breakdown in an attempt to reach a working consensus —which achieved what could not be achieved by consensus. Additionally, many problems of equal opportunity were dramatized by conflict. It is not necessary to further multiply examples; the point is that social conflict is a hard fact of social and organizational life, and the continued neglect of conflict in school systems leads to distorted interpretations and has an adverse effect on policy and planning by vitiating the ability of policymakers to understand organizations and to make reasonably accurate predictions about the effects of policy.

It is usually assumed in the equilibrium model that conflict, if it remains unchecked, will lead to disorganization and eventually the disintegration of the organization. Moreover, since conflict, by its very nature, is looked upon as a real threat to equilibrium, the social functions served by conflict are overlooked. According to Coser, conflict helps maintain the identity and boundary lines of groups. It develops ingroup and outgroup distinctions among group members and contributes to the group's sense of identity. Conflict often helps to maintain group relations providing an outlet for hostility among members, thereby making it unnecessary for them to withdraw because they feel badly thwarted. Conflict with outgroups also helps to establish greater internal cohesion within the group. As conflict ensues between two or more groups it affects the internal structure in terms of its tolerance for diversity of views and dissent. Conflicts with outgroups tend to define the types of internal conflict that will be tolerated.[26] Armies are less tolerant of dissent and conflict during wartime than during peacetime.

Churches that view themselves in conflict with other churches to win converts will be less tolerant than churches that do not militantly compete for converts.

Social conflict tends to redefine existing norms or establish new norms as applicable. During wartime, the set of norms applicable to the soldier differs from the ones that govern civil society; if this were not so, the soldier's acts would be felonious. In teachers' strikes, an attempt is made, if only implicitly, to redefine the teacher's rights in policy-making and in procedures for the redress of grievances. In other words, the thrust of a teachers' strike is to call into question substantive school-board or administrative policies and, at times, to challenge the legitimacy of the procedures. Frequently, new norms and policies emerge from such conflicts. This is not by any means the only way that new norms and policies can be created, but in view of the rigidity of some bureaucratic school systems, it may be the most probable way by which such changes can be brought about.

Any theory attempting to predict when conflict is likely to ensue would not only need to have sufficient data about past organizational behavior to develop initial hypotheses, but it would also need to take into account the fact that aggrieved parties who lack access to channels for the expression of grievances do not, for a variety of reasons, always precipitate conflict with organizational authorities. Moreover, when conflicts do develop, the reasons why they occur may not always seem to be "rational." To give reasons for behavior is a rational activity, but because it is rational does not mean that the activity cannot be used to explain behavior which is not rational (as Freud has shown). In spite of these difficulties, there is a great need for school systems to be studied in terms of conflict models; otherwise, the meaning of their activities will continue to be distorted. Additionally, a defensible theory of organizational change cannot be developed without the use of various models of social conflict.

A further word about organizational change. Many studies of organizational change in education are concerned with various ways in which innovations can be introduced in school systems. The structure of the system remains essentially unaffected while innovations are adopted. The fact that many of the most important changes stem from social conflict rather than the introduction of innovation is usually overlooked. Moreover, where bureaucratic school systems have become highly rigidified, conflict is probably the only way that new structural changes can be brought about. Before social-conflict models will be seriously entertained, however, educators must break the bewitchment spell that homeostasis, consensus, adaptation, equilibrium, and social control have cast.

Structural Changes for Individualizing Instruction

Recruitment and promotion policies pose problems for schools seeking to make structural changes that will facilitate greater individualization of instruction. Some school systems, as a result of their selection procedures, discourage the development of a diverse teaching staff. As Peter Schrag notes in his study of the Boston public schools, the types of examinations and point scales and the impersonal selection and promotion procedures tend to attract the same kind of people. The city's teacher examinations, given only in Boston and required of all candidates irrespective of experience, emphasize textbook questions based on the memorization of facts rather than critical thinking and the demonstration of creative abilities. The majority of the teachers attended the same public or parochial schools and graduated from the same colleges. They are predominantly of Irish lower-middle-class background and 99 percent are white.[27]

David Rogers's study of the New York City public schools also revealed considerable homogeneity of teaching staff due to inbreeding. This condition was attributed to the small effort made to recruit outside the city, examinations that stressed localized knowledge accessible only to insiders, and a system of "prepping" for the examinations that brought inside candidates under the tutelage of the administrative hierarchy.[28]

From recruitment conditions of the type found in Boston, New York, and some other metropolitan areas, a civil service attitude, rather than the appropriate professional attitude, develops toward teaching. This attitude impedes the considerable changes needed to bring about well-developed individualized instructional programs. Moreover, the homogeneity of the teaching staff allows little flexibility in testing new programs and developing new teaching approaches and classroom arrangements.

The second problem that militates against greater individualization of instruction lies in the promotion policies of most public school systems in the United States. The route by which the teacher seeks to advance himself is very limited and restricted in most public schools. There are no intermediate status-positions in teaching comparable to those found in other types of organizations. In some business firms the employee may eventually be able to advance from a stockroom clerk to sales manager or to a higher administrative position. To demonstrate abilities in teaching year after year leads no further than one's present position, except that there will very likely be salary increments. Too frequently, however, the same salary increments are awarded all tenured teachers who faithfully abide by administrative policies, irrespective of their actual effectiveness as teachers. The only "promotion" open to most teachers is to leave teaching for administrative positions. This lack of opportunity creates a dilemma for the good teacher: whether to remain in teaching (in spite of the general lack of differentiation in demonstrated teaching ability), become an administrator, or leave education altogether for a position in business or industry.

Both recruitment and promotion policies can be improved in such a way that teaching will be made more attractive as a career, rigid bureaucratization of schools can be curbed, and instruction can be more fully individualized. First, recruitment can be improved by schools deliberately seeking teachers from a wider diversity of geographical, social-class, racial, and minority-group backgrounds, and then giving the teachers greater autonomy—that is, the type of autonomy more consonant with professional status. Second, teachers should be treated as professionals. Third, school-district tests that screen out most everyone but those who can memorize well, tests that have little or no connection with teaching ability, should be eliminated. Fourth, the system should be decentralized so that teachers can have a hand in policy-making in their areas of competence and interest. Finally, there should be a graduated, flexible structure for promotion and advancement for career teachers.

Changing the opportunities for advancement in teaching would rest on the conviction that good teachers should no longer have to go into administration or leave education altogether in order to secure benefits correlative with achievement. In order to accomplish this large task, it will be necessary to create a number of paraprofessional, semiprofessional, and professional positions which are clearly differentiated from one another. It is well known that in most schools the teacher's schedule is organized in such a way that insufficient time is available for preparation, evaluation, individual work with students, and a host of other vital activities. As noted earlier, the growth of bureaucratic systems has led to the development of standardization, which, although at one time it served important purposes, has become too rigidified to allow for the flexible instructional patterns needed today. It is not being proposed that all standardization be eliminated; rather, standardization practices should be substantially modified and made much more highly flexible in the areas mentioned above.

Just as the use of nurses and orderlies in hospitals allows physicians to concentrate on using their specialized medical and surgical skills, the widespread employment of paraprofessionals in education would permit teachers to concentrate on the features of teaching that they are uniquely qualified to fulfill. A second reason for the use of paraprofessionals is that it would enable prospective teachers, through a period of employment early in their undergraduate education, to gain valuable first-hand experience in the schools and thereby determine more realistically whether they wish to pursue teaching as a career. Third, it would attract people from the community whose special abilities and interests remain largely untapped, many of whom might find serving as a paraprofessional personally rewarding. Finally, the paraprofessional level provides a route for promotion for those who later choose to return to college to complete their teaching certificate.

The number and types of paraprofessionals needed is debatable. Lloyd Bishop, in his study of individualizing instruction, differentiates four levels: clerical assistants and proctors; technical assistants and instructional assistants; instructional associates; and research assistants.[29] Each of these positions is differentiated from the others in terms of salary, formal educational requirements, and job description. Whether these particular positions or somewhat different types are needed is open to question. What should be evident at this point is that paraprofessionals have an important role to play in instructional and clerical responsibilities. Teachers do need to be relieved of clerical tasks, and arrangements should be made for the employment of qualified clerical assistants and proctors who can keep records, duplicate materials, collect funds, monitor students, and score simple objective tests. Teachers also need paraprofessionals who can work with small groups of students; supervise students in the library, playground, and lunchroom; maintain student records; monitor testing periods; help prepare instructional aids; handle various media for instructional purposes; and perform related tasks. Teachers need access to action-research findings which can be used in their classrooms. This means, ideally speaking, that all school systems should have full-time researchers who can work cooperatively with teachers in utilizing applicable research findings. Small school districts, as a start, should at least be able to employ a part-time researcher. Later, as demands for his services increase, a case can be made for staffing one or more full-time researchers.

Paraprofessional positions should be open to those who do not aspire to full-time teaching positions and to students who need experience in classroom situations. For the latter group, the experience of working as a paraprofessional will not only enrich their background for teaching but will also enable them to make a more realistic career choice prior to the completion of their undergraduate program. Rather than the usual haste to complete one's studies and get a teaching certificate, the staffing of schools with paraprofessionals will allow the prospective teacher to take off from formal study for one or more years by serving as a paraprofessional. In order that the turnover in these positions does not become excessive, administrators should also seek qualified persons who do not intend to become full-time teachers.

Bishop's plan for differential staffing of teaching consists of five different positions: intern teacher; probationary teacher; staff teacher; master teacher; and teacher specialist.[30] Although he does not make the distinction, the teaching faculty would consist of semiprofessionals and professionals. The first three positions, which can be found in a number of school systems, are most likely semiprofessionals. The intern teacher would be serving part-time or full-time for one year; the probationary teacher would be nontenured; and the staff teacher would be tenured with a fifth year of college study (not necessarily including the M.A. degree). These positions have different salary ranges and somewhat different functions based on qualifications.

The professional positions—master teacher and teacher specialist —would be unique as most systems are presently organized. The master teacher would hold an M.A. degree and have demonstrated ability to assume leadership in teaching. Duties would consist of assisting in the supervision of interns and probationary teachers; holding leadership positions on curriculum committees and faculty organizations; serving as team-teaching leader; and assisting in research projects. To assume, however, that the master teacher could offer some contribution to research projects would entail greater preparation in educational research at the M.A. level than is traditionally the case.

The teacher specialist would have post-master's-degree work or a doctorate (although it would be foolish to tie the position too closely with formal degree and course requirements if the teacher exhibits the requisite competencies). The responsibilities of the teacher specialist would consist of research in the area of specialization; consultation and demonstrations in the areas of competence; planning and coordinating systemwide programs; and performing in experimental teaching situations. It would appear, however, that the teacher specialist would serve only in a leadership and advisory role in coordinating systemwide programs; the day-to-day details can probably best be handled by the administration. A further qualification can be made about the research role. Assuming that full-time researchers are needed in every school district, the function of the teacher specialist will not only be to conduct research in his specialty but also to serve as a connecting link between the researcher and the total teaching faculty.

Each of these teaching positions is differentiated in salary scale, beginning at $7,500 for the intern and rising to $17,000–$25,000 for the teaching specialist on twelve months' service. (Of course these salary figures are only suggestive; the point to be remembered is that salaries must be differentiated on the basis of demonstrated competence.) Bishop has designated the percentage of teaching staff holding each of the respective positions: intern teachers (10 percent); probationary and staff teachers (65 percent); master teachers (20 percent); and teacher specialists (5 percent). Hopefully, the incentives of this plan will encourage larger proportions than those listed above to qualify as master teachers and teacher specialists.

For differential staffing to work, however, it will be necessary to dispense with the self-contained classroom as the basic arrangement for organizing instruction. Schools will have to break this lockstep pattern by utilizing several different forms of instructional organization and new scheduling arrangements. It will be necessary to use team teaching, large-group and small-group instruction, independent study, computer-assisted instruction, and other forms of instruction. Flexible scheduling will enable the schools to effectively utilize multiple forms of instruction. Rather than dividing the school day into conventional class periods, each of the same length, flexible units called "modules" of approximately twenty minutes in length are more adaptable because they can be used singly or in any number of combinations for instructional purposes. Classes may be scheduled using any number of modules, but classes may not necessarily be scheduled five days per week or at the same time as in present instructional arrangements. The use of modules allows the student to pursue a larger number of different courses and work within much more flexible time arrangements.

Changing Participation Patterns in Policy Formation

One of the characteristics of a profession is the relatively high degree of autonomy given its members. Professionals, as contrasted to other occupational groups, are expected to be more self-directing and capable of working independently of regular supervision. As a result of their advanced education, specialization, and highly developed skills, they not only are capable of exercising greater autonomy but are generally thought to need more autonomy in order to be more productive and creative.

If teaching is considered a profession, or at least an "emerging profession," the limited autonomy of teaching (except in some colleges and universities) is striking as compared to medicine and law. Although it may seem that this is not the case because teachers, once on tenure, are not highly supervised, it should be recognized, nonetheless, that teachers are usually granted little or no role in policy-making. By implication, teachers are thought to be incapable of playing a larger role in policy-making. The upshot of this condition is that teachers are hemmed in on all sides, in many school systems, by policies and regulations which limit their range of professional operations, policies which they are expected to comply with but which they had no hand in developing. This salient characteristic of teaching conditions today indicates that teachers lack the autonomy enjoyed by professionals.

But it could be counterargued that teaching is still not a profession, that at best it is semiprofessional in nature, and therefore teachers cannot be granted the full autonomy of professionals because they are not as yet capable of effectively handling such autonomy. Many proponents of this position would at least agree that teaching is becoming more professional and that over a period of time—the length of time is usually not specified—it will achieve full professional stature. The argument rests on the notion that one must first be fully a professional person before he can be given the autonomy befitting a professional position. But if teaching is semiprofessional and growing more professional, it would impede its professional progress if greater autonomy is not provided during this development process.

If it is granted, then, that teachers should be given more autonomy not only because it is appropriate for professionals and needed by those who are attempting to become more fully professional, but also for the reason that teachers have important ideas to contribute, especially in such areas as curriculum and instruction, the question of how these changes can be effected looms large. One of the chief problems lies in the very structure of bureaucratic school systems: until the structure is changed, it would appear that only limited progress will be made. Earlier it was pointed out that changes in the theoretical models would be needed; we still need to see what specific structural changes are necessary before the desired conditions can be fully implemented.

Many writers of late have criticized bureaucracies, but very few have offered alternative models. One exception to this trend can be found in the writings of Warren G. Bennis.[31] Among the causes of the predicted decline of bureaucracies, according to Bennis, first and foremost is the inability of bureaucracies to manage the tension and conflict between individual and management goals. Second is the revolutionary changes in science and technology and the growth of research and development. In terms of the latter cause, there will be an acceleration of the growing interdependence of business and government, leading to less competition, more turbulence, and large-scale organizations. The formal educational level of the total population will continue to increase and the tasks of organizations will become more technical and unprogrammed. Organizations will become more concerned with innovative and creative activities.

The social structure of organizations of the future, Bennis says, will be rapidly changing "temporary systems." Groups will be organized on the basis of problems-to-be-solved. Individuals will not be differentiated according to rank or status but in terms of abilities and professional training. The executive will become the force coordinating different task forces. This form of social organization, which he calls an "organic-adaptive" structure, involves the use of specialized talents in a team arrangement to attack specific problems. Since the teams will be short-lived, this poses the problem of the lack of the more enduring relations that are characteristic of present bureaucracies. This means that more flexible and adaptable individuals, skilled in human relations, will be needed. One of the tasks of education in the future will be to teach individuals how to live with the strains and the lack of group cohesiveness of such organizations. The theme of living in a world of rapid change is not a new one, but it takes on new significance as we view possible forms of social organization in occupations of the future.

Some of the organizational changes first forecasted by Bennis in the mid-1960s are already manifested in varying degrees in professional and research organizations and in the aerospace, drug, construction, and consulting industries. The strict allegiance to the hierarchy is eroding as specialists work together in a chain-of-command that no longer can wait for approval at a higher level before taking action. The new type of organizational individual must assume responsibility for decision-making. The stability and permanence associated with bureaucracies yields to a short-lived, more intense relationship that calls for persons with highly developed abilities who can work together as a team and make independent decisions. The team concept may also be extended to administration, since some administrative tasks are too complex for any single individual to handle successfully. Administrators will increasingly have to be chosen for, among other qualifications, their ability to work as members of a team. A proper blending of skills and abilities will be needed in order to make a viable team. The incentives in such organizations will revolve more around humanistic values and self-actualization than material gain.

Bennis's organic-adaptive model is consonant with the need of professionals for greater autonomy. Applying the model to school systems, it is immediately apparent that existing hierarchical structures and lines of authority militate against greater autonomy and a larger role for teachers in policy-making. The administration should recognize that teachers are uniquely prepared to share the responsibilities for policy development and evaluation in the areas of curriculum and instruction. The principal, while frequently looked upon as the instructional leader of the school, should reconceptualize his role as a collaborative one. Lloyd Bishop has suggested that greater participation and autonomy can be brought about by establishing a "professional teacher core."[32] The core would consist of both teachers in the various disciplines and teachers with interdisciplinary responsibilities; although there would be some similarity with team teaching, more flexibility and overlapping of team members would be found. Some of the teams would be temporary task forces, which would be established to attack specific problems. The teams would be formed by the professional teacher core in response to curricular problems that require solution.

Bishop recommends that a "composite principalship task-force team" be organized to provide leadership and help coordinate and implement decisions of the professional teacher core. This task force consists of the principal, co-principal, or multiprincipal team, and curriculum associates. In this schema, the multiprincipal team's primary concerns are with the coordination of curriculum and instruction rather than chiefly with administration and public relations. The curriculum associates consist of outstanding teachers with the expertise to provide leadership and direction in curriculum development. These associates would still spend part of their time teaching and working with students. The curriculum associate is a specialist in one area of the curriculum, whereas the principal unit is composed of generalists. The curriculum associate is the coordinator or linchpin between the principal unit and the professional teacher core.

The type of organic-adaptive model would likely provide the greater autonomy and participation needed by teachers. Whether this model or a modification of it is used, it is important that teachers be given more responsibility in policy-making. For instance, in a study by Francis Chase, four hundred teachers from various parts of the country were interviewed in regard to their attitudes on policy-making.[33] He found that teachers who participated regularly in policy-making, such as in the areas of curriculum, pupil personnel, and teacher salaries, were more likely to be enthusiastic and hold positive attitudes toward their school system. Teachers in schools where salaries were low were more likely to resent the lack of opportunity to participate in the determination of salary schedules than teachers in systems where salaries are high. Conversely, those who participate are less likely to blame the administration for low salaries than those who do not participate.

While Chase recommends that teachers should have an opportunity to participate in those matters in which they are most interested, it would be more appropriate to expand the criterion to include the qualification of competence. Interest and competence do not always coincide, for teachers may have interests in some areas of the school's program, such as counseling or schedule programming, where they lack competence; and they are likely to have competence in curriculum development but may lack interest because of heavy schedules and other pressures.

The following conclusions can be drawn. First of all, teachers' attitudes toward their school system usually become more positive when they participate more widely in policy-making. Second, professionals need greater autonomy and more freedom to make decisions that affect their work and well-being. Third, since present bureaucratic school systems severely limit the teacher's role in this area, a decentralized organic-adaptive model, as outlined above, should be widely tested. Fourth, differential staffing, as mentioned earlier, will be needed in order for the model to work. Finally, it is hypothesized that when these four conditions are met, schools will more readily and efficaciously fulfill their goals.

CHAPTER 5

The Politics of Policy Development

After examining policy operations in their organizational setting in the last chapter, we now turn our attention to policy within a larger social and political context and examine the forces which influence and shape it. More specifically, in this chapter we will first examine the procedures actually used in policy-making. We will then turn our attention to determining what bodies and agencies, official or otherwise, are vested with the responsibility for policy development. This is closely related to the next topic, how policies are implemented and the political forces involved in the process. Finally, the chapter closes with a reassessment of policy-making.

HOW POLICY IS MADE

Scholars have proposed a number of models, either of policy-making or decision-making, for the improvement of policy. These models are designed to simulate rational modes of thought and the procedure to be followed in the development of policy. In Chapter 2, we reviewed the connection of decision-making theory to policy development to ascertain whether the theory could be used for developing policy. To recapitulate, decision-making theory seeks to determine the most efficient and effective course of action among various alternatives in a situation through the use of a system for making optimal decisions. "Optimality" is based on the relative value of various outcomes which are likely to accrue from different choices. It was shown that a maximizing model is inappropriate and unrealistic because it seeks the best alternatives rather than an alternative that will reasonably satisfy the policy-makers' aspiration level at a particular time. Additionally, decision-making theory fails to consider irrationality and unconscious or partly conscious motives in the policy-making process.

Braybrooke and Lindblom have discussed two other models developed by social scientists: the rational-deductive ideal and the welfare function.[1] Although we will not go into the details of these models here, the authors contend that no one has actually been able to construct such models in a workable form for policy analysis. After pointing up numerous shortcomings of these models, they argue that "disjointed incrementalism" is a commonplace strategy in policy analysis; and they seek to show how this strategy can be refined for the improvement of policy-making. The strategy of disjointed incrementalism applies to ordinary political life, in which decisions effect small changes and are made with limited understanding and assessment of the problems and variables involved.[2] Large-scale changes, they believe, are infrequent; and it is rare for the policy-maker to have a synoptic understanding of the multiplicity of variables involved in a policy situation. The major features of disjointed incrementalism are: (1) focusing only on increments by which the outputs of policy differ from one policy to another; (2) consideration of a restricted variety of policy alternatives, excluding those entailing radical change; (3) consideration of a restricted number of consequences for any one policy; (4) adjustment of objectives to policies as well as policies to objectives; (5) formulation of the problem as data become available; (6) choosing among policies by ranking the increments by which they differ.[3]

As noted earlier, this strategy is unsuited to large-scale changes and to cases where there is a high degree of understanding of situation variables. The strategy is probably most useful where policy-makers seek limited objectives and are not faced with crisis conditions which demand large-scale decisions or a reconstruction of the policy network. Moreover, Braybrooke and Lindblom offer little or no empirical evidence to demonstrate that this strategy is actually the way policies are made.

There are a number of other considerations that should be taken into account in determining how policy is made. The first thing to recognize is the constraints under which policy-makers operate. These constraints include time, information, resources, personality limitations of the policy-makers, institutional rules and expectations, uncertainty, and risk. The importance of each factor can be briefly mentioned. The policy-maker does not have unlimited time; time is at a premium in many cases and therefore policy decisions must be made with less information, planning, and deliberation than ideally desirable. Considerable time periods are needed when complex policy decisions are to be made; but in simpler decisions deadlines may be useful to goad those who tend to procrastinate. Some persons, however, do not work best under deadlines; thus this is a personality factor which should be considered when setting up a policy-making team.

All policy-makers must operate with insufficient information. Even with large amounts of time (which a policy-maker rarely has), not all information needed can be obtained. There is still insufficient knowledge as to which type of systems are most conducive to policy change, nor can we be certain as to the specific conditions under which proposed new policies are most likely to be accepted. Furthermore, policy-making is future-oriented in regard to both long-term and short-term outcomes, but the present ability of the social sciences to predict policy outcomes with a high degree of probability is quite limited. The need for assessing the multiple and complex variables in a policy situation poses acute information needs for the policy maker. But, because of the constraints of time, information, and other factors, as we have seen from the criticisms of decision-making theory, there is no way at present to optimize policy making. Moreover, even in some cases where the time factor is not overly restrictive in limiting the gathering of knowledge and information, limited resources may preclude doing so. Thus, by the very nature of his task the policy-maker must make choices on the basis of limited information. In spite of these considerable difficulties, he still has a responsibility to make the wisest decisions possible under the circumstances.

The policy-maker has at his disposal the resources of physical goods, money, and manpower. Also, in a sense, the personality factors and competencies of the policy-making team can be classified as resources. Resources are always scarce, not only because they are never unlimited but because resources rarely match the dreams and ideals of men. Almost any program, whether in government, industry, or education, can use greater resources. A critical factor for policy-makers is their ability to acquire more resources; but it is also vital that they make wise use of the resources they already have. Resources serve as constraints in the sense of setting the definable limits of how and what can be done. On the other hand, policy-makers who lack imagination and foresight are unable to make maximum use of the available resources. Personal resources, which consist of the personality and abilities of policy-makers and the personnel who execute policy, are other important variables. The personal skills of policy-makers—persuasiveness, tactical skills, and bargaining abilities—are vital ingredients in policy-making. The situation, role expectations, and personal skills of the policy-maker influence which set of policies will prevail.

The institutional rules and regulations place limits on the type and thrust of policies which can be approved at any given time. Large bureaucratic school systems have an enormous number of rules and regulations that confine policy-makers who think of policy development in terms of disjointed incrementalism. Those who seek to bring about considerable change in the system may need, in some cases, to make wholesale changes in rules and regulations. We have been speaking, however, about internal rules established by the system itself. There are also numerous external policies that school systems must abide by, principally those from state departments of education and those attached to federal educational programs.

Policy-makers also face uncertainty and risk. Since predictability of policy outcomes is not high, there is always uncertainty. There is almost invariably a lack of certitude whether a set of approved policies are the right ones for a particular set of conditions, a given time period, and existing personnel. Risks are not only a function of the level of uncertainty but of the possible scope and impact of a policy. In other words, if a policy is designed to make small, incremental changes in an organization and the uncertainty level is high, the risks are not as great as a policy with a relatively higher certainty level but broad in scope and intended to bring about significant and far-reaching changes. Not only is the latter type of policy likely to meet with far greater resistance, but even if the policy has the support of a majority of the personnel, its failure is likely to bring about serious repercussions, especially in cases where expectations are high. Hence, this is another of the many reasons why policy-makers have a proclivity for taking small, incremental steps.

Not all policy-makers use disjointed incrementalism or some similar step-by-step procedure in arriving at decisions. They may only use rules of thumb, relying on their own personal experiences and intuitions. In the face of uncertainty, they may consult with experts, especially where policy decisions involve technical matters. Another way to reduce uncertainty is to send up "trial balloons" to detect possible reactions to contemplated proposals. Policy-makers attempt to sound out personnel and key public officials to test receptivity to proposals. And occasionally public-opinion surveys are conducted. Attempts are also made to determine more precisely the causal relations between processes and outcomes; however, the present state of the social sciences does not permit precise determination. In light of these difficulties, it is not surprising that policy-makers often delay decisions until uncertainty diminishes appreciably. But when delays are lengthy or a prompt decision is sorely needed, the policy-maker may be accused of vacillation and indecisiveness. Nevertheless, the policy-maker is genuinely reluctant to commit himself to a policy which may appear to be precipitous or whose outcomes may prove embarrassing.

Some policies have long-run predictions of promised benefits but may not be undertaken because the public is oriented toward quick, tangible benefits. The public may become impatient with policy-makers who use large amounts of resources to bring about distant, though significant, changes. This situation is usually the case in politics and obtains only to a slightly lesser extent in the area of educational policy-making.

Before making new policies, it is also necessary to calculate the more immediate outcomes of existing policy; however, as we have seen, this is difficult to do. A knowledge is needed of the effects of policy and the changes likely to be produced. Although change is constantly taking place, the rate of change is uneven. During some exceptional periods change is very rapid, whereas change is usually fairly slow for considerable periods of time. Rapid change may be precipitated by a crisis in the system, either of internal or external origin. A far-reaching decision may also precipitate a period of more rapid change not fully foreseen, as in the *Brown* v. *Board of Education of Topeka* decision. In the face of rapid change, the tendency is usually to minimize risks by delaying decisions until the general drift and consequences of sudden changes can be determined. On the other hand, a few policy-makers view periods of rapid change as an opportunity to maximize gains by taking risks in the face of uncertainty.

The Planning Process

One way by which uncertainty and risk can be appreciably diminished is for policy-makers to engage in systematic planning. Planning enables the policy-making team to assess its resources and to analyze the variables that are most likely to influence policy decisions and their implementation. Without systematic planning, especially in the case of complex policy decisions, risk, uncertainty, and the likelihood of failure are increased.

Before planning can get underway, there first must be a sense of awareness, a recognition of need that there should be some change in policy. The change could be to rescind or modify an existing policy, or to establish a new policy. The need for such changes is determined in various ways. The outcomes of a policy or set of related policies may not have met expectations; consequently, a reassessment of the source of the problem must be made. Data can be collected and studies conducted to assess policy operations. In some cases, grievances of personnel and social conflicts within the system may bring attention to the need to reevaluate the impact of present policies. New demands may also be placed upon local school systems by outside agencies. For instance, state departments of education, in their examination of local school districts, may find that they fail to comply with certain state-approved standards. In like manner, the U.S. Office of Education can withhold federal aid until a school district meets the required standards. In such cases the need to reexamine policy becomes preeminent. While there are numerous other ways whereby policy-makers recognize the need to reexamine policy, the point is that no changes are undertaken without such a recognition and a willingness to act upon it.

Once the need for making changes in policy is recognized, it then becomes necessary to gather data which bear upon the problem at hand and can be used in helping the policy leader to make intelligent choices among the various alternatives open to him. If the problem is not overly complex, a committee can be organized and responsibilities can be assigned for gathering pertinent information. With effective organization and the appointment of qualified persons, the information can be gathered quickly and placed in a form that will be of maximum usefulness to policy-makers. On the other hand, more complex decisions require more extensive information and research into the problem to uncover all the many relevant factors and variables. Among the different forms of data that may need to be acquired are findings from action research, school testing programs, educational research, surveys and reports from state and federal governments, school records and reports, and data from observations and interviews.[4] In order to secure information from these various sources, the task cannot be turned over to a committee; it is necessary to appoint qualified researchers to gather the needed evidence. Hence, it is important for school systems to have full-time researchers.

After the necessary information has been gathered and organized it is then necessary to interpret the data. The interpretation of the data may show that further information is needed, or that some of the information obtained is incorrect. The researcher's services are still required at this stage of planning in order to interpret specialized findings and present them to the policy-making unit. Since policy-makers are not always well versed in research design and methodology, it is incumbent upon the researcher to communicate his findings in clear, nontechnical language. The researcher also plays a role in evaluating findings in terms of their probable bearing upon the problem with which the policy-makers are concerned. It is then the responsibility of policy-makers to determine how the findings can help them plan more effectively. This is usually accomplished by a further assessment of the relevance of the data to the problem under consideration, and by sorting out and sifting those findings which can best be used in carrying out their objectives.

In light of the data and the knowledge of the situation which they provide, the next step is to examine the various alternatives available. As we indicated earlier in this chapter, the numerous constraints on the policy-making process make it certain that the alternatives will never be unlimited. The attempt to locate criteria for optimizing conditions is not feasible (as was shown in Chapter 2). Rather, it was proposed by Herbert Simon that a "satisficing" model is more suitable for policy-makers. This model, as will be recalled, is based on search activities to meet certain aspiration levels rather than on problem-solving, which involves finding the best alternatives in terms of specific criteria. Because of the constraints of the situation and the inability to assess all of the multiplicity of variables and the numerous possible alternatives involved in a complex decision, the satisficing model for appraising alternatives is more suited to the policy-making process.

If a policy, or set of policies, is made by the administration without the participation of teachers and other educational personnel, the task of communicating and implementing new policies or changes in existing policies may be acute. This is especially true when the system is a large bureaucracy and teachers do not participate and are not consulted prior to the making of policy decisions. In this case the central administration must establish effective contact with the different subsystems lower in the hierarchy, explain the purpose and scope of the policies, and establish guidelines for implementation and evaluation. As the distance between the policy-makers and the targeted areas increases, the likelihood of a breakdown in communication is heightened. This means, then, that the channels of communication must remain open, both down and up the hierarchy, to provide the necessary input and feedback. As policies and the plans by which they are to be implemented become more comprehensive and complex, greater difficulties are likely to be experienced in effective communication. But when those who are most directly affected by the policies are involved in their determination, a number of these problems of communication and implementation are likely to be alleviated.

It may therefore be necessary for policy-makers to treat communication as a specific problem in the planning stage. In that way they can focus more attention on the abilities of the communicator and the communicatee, on the forms of policy statements that are more likely to be understood, and on the uses and availability of media to enhance the communication process. Thus one component of the plan should be devoted to communication, especially when proposed policies are comprehensive and complex and also when they have been developed without teacher participation. Hence, it would be a serious mistake to believe that communication will take care of itself; rather, a conscious effort must be made in the planning stage to consider all salient difficulties that may be encountered in communication and thereby to devise various strategies by which these anticipated problems are most likely to be resolved.

Acceptance and Resistance to Change

The successful implementation of policy is dependent not only on an effective communications network, but also on the willingness of personnel to accept change. The act of rescinding, modifying, or establishing a new policy always brings change to persons falling within the scope of the policy's application; and though observers have frequently apprised others that change is an endemic feature of our time, resistance to policy changes is still commonly found. The reasons for this resistance are not too hard to divine. Changes in social institutions, organizations, and associations differ in scope, extensiveness, and rapidity; some areas of organizational life remain relatively constant while others are changing. But all the talk about change almost leaves one with the impression that everything is changing at once—which obviously is not true; if it were true, there would be widespread disorganization and even chaos in some quarters. The fact that we have a notion of change assumes some point of stability in relation to which the concept of change gets its meaning.

Turning more specifically to the tendency of many people to resist change, a host of reasons can be cited, reasons which the policy-maker should be fully cognizant of. It has already been mentioned that the likelihood of resistance to change is greater when teachers do not participate or have a voice in policy decisions, especially when they believe that they possess the competencies to make a contribution in the particular policy area. There is always some resistance to change when those affected disapprove of the new policies, the changes new policy will bring about, or both. A distinction can be made between agreement or disagreement with a policy and approval or disapproval of its consequences. A group of teachers may agree with the policy that there should be regular and systematic contact between teachers and parents, but they may disapprove of the consequences of the policy if it is interpreted to mean that teachers must return to school two nights per week in order to meet with parents. On the other hand, a teacher may not fully approve of a policy that discriminates against certain teachers on the basis of race or religion, but he may approve of the consequences of the policy if he stands to benefit because he is not of that race or religion. In other words, he may state that the policy is actually discriminatory, but since people in this world must first look after themselves, it would be against his personal interests to fight for its repeal.

Another explanation why a policy may be resisted is that those most directly affected do not understand the thinking behind the policy, the reasons that can be adduced for its support. The policy-makers may have deliberately withheld this information, or carelessly overlooked the need to present it, or else they attempted to present it, but the communications network was not functioning effectively. Whatever the source of the problem, once a plausible rationale is proffered, personnel will understand the reasons for the policy and will seek to voluntarily comply with it. This explanation may apply in some cases; it breaks down, however, by relying exclusively on the notion that man is strictly a rational being. But it is also well known, according to Freud and other observers, that man is motivated by unconscious forces, which are not always understood and are not necessarily under the control of the actor. It is also the case that people frequently react to others in terms of stereotypes even though the stereotypes have no basis in fact. Moreover, it is common for persons to act on the basis of emotions, feelings, and impulses rather than reason. And, in addition, many human beliefs are based on faith, intuition, or just a desire to believe.

Evidence could be multiplied on both sides of the question, Is man essentially rational or irrational—or, perhaps, nonrational? There is a tendency for some to seek a rock-bottom principle that will explain all of human behavior. But to do so is to ignore the richness, variety, and complexity of human life, as well as to disregard counterevidence. There is no sufficient reason, either logically or empirically, to assume that man must be one or the other; the evidence seems to indicate that he exhibits both tendencies at various times. And doubtlessly historical evidence could be presented to show that although rationality has been heightened in science and technology, changes of comparable magnitude have yet to occur in social and political relations. The point of this discussion is that we should not seek a single underlying factor to explain human motivation, but rather should recognize that multiple factors exist and that these factors should be considered by policy-makers who would like to overcome resistance to change.

Looking at man more in terms of his affective side, it is known that he lives by a set of values even though the values may not be fully conscious or consistent with one another. The fact that policy decisions reinforce and conflict with teachers' values gives a clue to the conflicts and forces of resistance which arise. In the planning stage, an assessment of possible sources of value conflicts should be undertaken so that these conflicts can be avoided whenever possible, and when they cannot be avoided, the groundwork should be laid to minimize them. Although significant institutional change may arise from value conflicts, it is not necessarily in the policy-maker's interest to precipitate these conflicts because it is difficult to keep conflict situations under control, as well as to have any assurance as to their possible outcomes. (In speaking of the use of conflict in the last chapter, our point of view was that of the rank and file or those outside the system who would generate conflicts in the hope of changing rigid, recalcitrant bureaucracies.)

Whenever an individual's values or interests are threatened, he is likely to resist the policies which he perceives as provoking the threat. There are also established habits and routines in work from which an individual derives a sense of continuity and stability. When these routines are disturbed by new policies, the individual is likely to become resistant and uncooperative. Thus, under conditions where there is some conflict with values and interests or where routines and established practices are disturbed, the groundwork must first be laid prior to the changes themselves if the policy is to be accepted. Principals, supervisors, and curriculum consultants should have an understanding of teachers' values so that they can anticipate policies which are likely to prove threatening and can work with teachers to modify their values and attitudes in light of policy changes. Of course the problem may lie not with the teachers but with the policy-makers: the latter's policies may, for one reason or another, be undesirable.

Assuming for the moment that the policies are needed and desirable but that their successful implementation is impeded by teachers, the policy-maker must be aware in the planning stage of the values, interests, attitudes, and routines of teachers and of how new policies or changes in older policies are likely to pose conflicts or cause disturbances. When new policies call for changes in habits and routines, teachers must be given a period in which they are free to adapt, explore, and make mistakes. During this period the groundwork should be laid for new patterns of behavior, and immediate thoroughgoing changes should not be demanded.

In some cases, however, the purpose of new policies is to reorganize the system on a different organizational basis. Policy-makers will usually recognize that changes of this magnitude will affect many vested interests and create many status anxieties. Realizing that a thoroughgoing reorganization is not likely to take place through voluntary adaptations during an extended period of planning, policy-makers are likely to take quick and massive action before resistance becomes widespread. A case in point was the widespread reorganization of the U.S. Office of Education during the Keppel administration.[5] In this case a number of vested interests were disrupted and some were destroyed.

Since complete reorganizations of educational systems are infrequent, our concern is with the orderly change process brought about by changing or abolishing old policies and establishing new ones. The policy-maker and his staff must determine the extent to which resistance is due to a lack of knowledge about the policy and its underlying purpose or, on the other hand, to a conflict in values, interests, and established routines. Only through planning is it likely that resistance will be minimized and cooperation enlisted.

WHO MAKES POLICY?

In order to improve policy-making it is necessary to know who makes policy and some of the important factors that influence these decisions. It is well known that the chief policy-making body at the local level is the school board. There have been a number of studies of the composition of school boards and the factors that influence their decisions. Some of the findings of these studies will be presented in order to clarify present policy-making at the local level.

There is considerable evidence that school-board members are not representative of a cross-section of their community but are composed mainly of certain business and professional interests. In an early study of school boards, George Counts reviewed several thousand school-board members and reported that three-fourths of them were business and professional men.[6] Social-stratification studies of communities also support these findings. Lloyd Warner and his associates found that business and professional men constituted about 75 percent of school-board membership in cities and towns, and, as expected, farmers composed the membership of rural boards.[7] In a study of Elmstown's schools, August Hollingshead found that school-board members represented different business, property, and professional interests.[8] School boards are overwhelmingly Anglo-Saxon Protestant, and manual and skilled workers total only about 2.4 percent in large urban districts.[9]

Does public-school policy, then, reflect the social-class interests of the business and professional groups who predominate on school boards? While observers agree on the matter of school-board composition, some do not believe that policies reflect the interests of a particular social class or occupational group. Roald Campbell studied the records of 172 school-board members in twelve Western cities from 1931 1940.[10] He found that in some instances there was no relationship between social status and conservative attitudes toward education; in other instances, the higher educational and occupational levels correlated with relatively liberal attitudes. It may be the case that the office imposes upon the board member certain wider community responsibilities that he would not assume in his private role as an individual citizen. One other explanation is that some group members do not always adhere to the norms of their group. However, these persons would very likely be exceptions, and the explanation would not be sufficient to account for Campbell's findings.

Perhaps a better approach is to recognize that those with more years of formal education show greater tolerance, and that larger amounts of education are related to a lowering of prejudice.[11] On the other hand, the higher the socioeconomic status, the more conservative the voting behavior.[12] There is some evidence that with the large proportion of business and managerial groups on school boards, some boards are interested in having the schools follow a business model in their operations.[13] Whether boards are essentially liberal or conservative, however, is difficult to determine, especially because such terms are slippery. While it is claimed that some boards have supported the teaching of religion in public schools or have maintained segregated schooling, it could possibly also be claimed that they were fulfilling the will of the community. Or possibly they were a moderating force in the face of more extreme groups.

Still, the fact that the public schools reflect middle-class values and all these values entail, that schools, for the most part, have been slow in adapting themselves to the needs of culturally different learners and frequently have failed to achieve genuine integration, is all the more reason why boards should represent a cross-section of the community. At least the voices of minority groups would have a better platform from which to be heard. Moreover, those who have taken the brunt of discrimination are far more sensitive in ferreting out policies which may be discriminatory.

Besides more proportionate representation on boards, what other desirable characteristics should we look for in school-board members? Neal Gross's study of school boards in Massachusetts throws some light on this question.[14] He used the evaluation of school superintendents of the motives of board members because the superintendent could be more objective and also describe motives related to the behavior of board members. Of the motives board members gave for seeking election, Gross considers "civic duty" as a "good" motive, and motives based on a desire to "represent some group" or "gain political experience" as "bad" motives. The latter two were considered undesirable motives because the desire to represent some group is more likely to contribute to that group's benefit than to the benefit of the total school population; and because "political experience" is likely to contribute to the individual's personal interests and advancement and only incidentally to the school as a whole.

Gross found no relationship between occupation and "good" motivation. Thus, the business and managerial groups which dominate school boards have no greater proportion of good motivation than other occupational groups. Years of formal schooling, sex, and marital status make little difference in motivation. It was found that members with children have relatively more good motivation than members without children. Additionally, school-board members from age forty to sixty-five are likely to have better motivation than young adults and more elderly members. Moreover, the longer members have served on the board, the greater likelihood that their motivation will be "good." The analysis revealed that the higher the proportion of board members motivated by civic duty, the greater the likelihood of a consensus on their role and that of the superintendent.

Is community power organized in such a manner that those who make policy decisions on public school matters also make the key decisions in other vital areas of community life? Observers disagree. Some studies show that power is essentially monolithic in the sense that an elite makes most of the community decisions;[15] other investigators take a more pluralistic position in their conclusion that power is more widely shared—those who make decisions in one area are not usually the decision-makers in other areas.[16] The different conclusions may, at least in part, stem from differences in basic assumptions and research designs.

In a study of four suburban school districts, Bloomberg and Sunshine found that, with rare exceptions, school-board members participated in no other areas of community decision-making.[17] Various citizens provided input into the policy-making process; the average number of participants in school policy decisions ranged from eight to sixteen. The informal decision-makers who were not board members ranged from one to seven in the four communities and participated in only a few decisions. Thus, this particular study failed to find a monolithic power structure controlling both community affairs and public school policy.

Returning to the subject of school-board composition, it should be noted that there have been studies of college and university boards of trustees. Earlier studies indicated that regents for state universities principally represented the upper-upper and lower-upper classes.[18] More recently, Rodney T. Hartnett of the Educational Testing Service conducted two studies that included trustees at five hundred colleges and universities.[19] He found that trustees consider themselves "moderate" Republicans, more than half of them have incomes of over $30,000, most are business executives, and the average trustee is a white male Protestant in his fifties, with one-third of those sampled over sixty. Conservatism was characteristic on matters of academic freedom, especially in the Southern and Rocky Mountain institutions. More than half of the trustees favored loyalty oaths for faculty members, and more than two-thirds were in favor of screening campus speakers. The trustees also favored a hierarchical system of decision-making.

OUTSIDE INFLUENCES ON LOCAL POLICY-MAKING

The State System and Its Authority over Local School Districts

In what ways does the state constrain, modify, or alter policy-making decisions at the local level? To answer this question, it should first be recognized that education today is essentially a state function. This was not always the case, however. The state's role in education began to grow during the late nineteenth century, but it was not until this century that state government assumed its primary role in public education. The growth of the state's role has come about for a number of reasons, including dereliction in local responsibility and the need to assure minimum standards, eliminate irregularities and erratic local practices, and secure a more equitable financial base.

The state regulates compulsory attendance, minimum length of school term, certification of teachers, and accreditation (in conjunction with regional accrediting bodies); establishes curriculum guidelines; provides financial aid; and exercises the power of establishing and abolishing school districts. These far-reaching powers indicate clearly and convincingly that education is a state function. Of course many policy-making functions are reserved to local districts, the extent depending in part upon the tightness or leniency of the state in fulfilling its jurisdictional functions.

Space does not permit a full description of the state's legislative and policy-making operations in education and of the internal politics involved. Our concern lies with the influence and impact of the state on policy-making at the local level.

The state has the power to shape policy on all of its educational functions listed above, as well as many less significant functions. The diligence with which it pursues and enforces these policy matters depends especially upon the particular state and the vigor with which state educational officials have carried out their duties.

There are certain generic similarities among the states, even though the details of policy and practice may differ considerably. The Tenth Amendment to the U.S. Constitution left to the states the right to organize and regulate public education. Legislatures have the authority, as granted by state constitutions, to regulate school districts and to establish laws governing educational matters. Serving as a state legislator is a part-time job, and legislators do not have the visibility of congressmen. In many states educational legislation does not attract as much public attention as other issues, and it generally is not considered as critical a matter as other issues during elections. As a result, education, generally speaking, is not a top priority. (There are, of course, some notable exceptions; for example, the situation in California during the 1960s.) School legislation is of two types: mandatory and permissive. Mandatory legislation covers a wide variety of areas: compulsory attendance, certification, maximum tax-rate permitted, teacher contracts, composition and responsibilities of local school boards, required budgets and audits, and other areas. Permissive legislation may pertain to the local board's power to borrow on anticipated revenues, school-district mergers, and sick-leave provisions. Some legislation is designed to establish minimum standards, such as the length of school terms, salaries, and others. Whereas mandatory laws state what must be done at the local level, permissive legislation and minimum standards permit experimentation and diverse policies.

State administration of education is conducted by a state board of education, the state superintendent of education, and the state department of education. Considerable diversity exists among the states in terms of board composition, basis of membership, size, and length of term. In more than half the states, all board members, or a majority of them, are appointed by the governor; in other states members are either elected, appointed by the legislature, named by local school-board members, or constituted ex officio. The size of the state boards ranges from three to twenty members, and the length of the terms from one to six years. The functions of the state boards are to execute education laws and to make appropriate policies of their own. Even in the case of state laws, the board, in many cases, can still determine specific policies. For example, the legislature, in establishing a general law for teacher certification, may grant jurisdiction of the specific requirements to the board. The board may also initiate such policies of its own as a statewide testing program, and it may establish length of school term, determine which school districts should be consolidated, and perform other functions. In most cases the board governs education in a general way and turns over the details and the execution of policy to the state department of education. The board, however, may supervise more than elementary and secondary schools; in about one-third of the states the board assumes authority for public colleges and universities.

The commissioner of education is considered the chief state school officer. He is appointed by the state board of education in twenty-four states, elected by popular vote in twenty-one and appointed by the governor in five states. The term of office is usually four years; and though in some states the term is only two years, there is a tendency to give the superintendent indefinite tenure in states where he is appointed by the board of education. The superintendent is the executive officer of the board of education and, in keeping with state laws and the policies of the board, he exercises general supervision of the state's public schools and organizes and directs the state department of education. The scope of the superintendent's authority depends, to a considerable extent, on the degree to which the position is not involved in party politics and is made an attractive one and given sufficient professional status so that more outstanding educators can be recruited. In many states, however, pay and prestige are low and the position is not filled by a prominent educator.

The day-by-day execution of state education policies is conducted by the state department of education, which sees that local school districts carry out state policies and fulfill state standards. This is frequently accomplished by means of surveys and on-the-spot inspection teams. With the state board's approval, the superintendent selects a staff of specialists best qualified to administer the special divisions and subunits of the state department. Unfortunately, in a number of states appointees are chosen for political reasons rather than professional competence. The staff size varies considerably in the different states, with staffs of only about fifty in some states and nearly two thousand in several; the average size is about two hundred.

Returning to our original question, In what ways does the state constrain, modify, or alter policy-making decisions at the local level? It is evident by now that the state has authority over local school districts. The extent to which the states exercise their powers and enforce their authority, of course, varies considerably; and the extent to which local school districts attempt to evade those state policies which they oppose depends in part on the rigorousness with which the state is prepared to enforce its policies. But even in states where policies are rigorously enforced, local school boards are still permitted to make policies applicable to their particular situation, as long as these policies are not violations of, or in conflict with, those of the state. Still, the ultimate jurisdiction of public education rests with the state.

Other State and Regional Influences

It was mentioned earlier that voters have an influence on the legislative process. Issues of considerable concern to voters, especially issues critical enough to influence the outcome of elections, are likely to be given top priority by the legislature. If public education is not in the public eye in a given state, education legislation will probably be given far less attention than issues on which public consciousness is more greatly sensitized. In fact, needed educational legislation may be bypassed or neglected during a session.

The state teachers' association, usually an affiliate of the National Education Association, has been a vocal and influential professional group in some states, especially in the Midwest, where membership is large and there is less competition with the American Federation of Teachers. In this section of the country, the state association collects much valuable information about the public schools and can supply selected information to legislators in order to get them to support a particular piece of legislation. This phenomenon has been referred to by some critics as further evidence of the strength exercised by the "educational establishment."[20] Thus, in some Midwestern states the state teachers' association has considerably more influence on the legislature than the National Education Association does on the Congress.

The regional accrediting associations are another policy-making group whose influence should not be overlooked. They have exercised an important influence on the standards of schools and colleges, and these institutions have eagerly sought to maintain accredited status lest their high school graduates encounter considerable difficulty in gaining admission to leading colleges and universities (this problem, however, seems to be abating somewhat with the increase in reliance by admissions officers on College Board examinations). Accredited standing is also eagerly sought by colleges. The regional accrediting associations, of which the North Central Association is by far the largest, establish only minimum standards. The accrediting associations have been criticized on the ground that only schools and colleges which are "scandalously inferior" are refused accreditation.[21] Furthermore, they have also been criticized for their failure to discriminate between the best and the

worst institutions because some of those accredited are, at best, medi-
ocre; and also on the ground that some of the accrediting standards are
vague and questionable.[22] Nevertheless, in spite of these criticisms
there has not been very much change in the standards and operating
procedures of the accrediting associations; and they still exert a large
degree of influence over educational programs and policies.

Federal and National Influences

The U.S. Constitution, through the Tenth Amendment, left to the
states the conduct of organized schooling; however, the section of the
Constitution that empowers Congress to collect taxes for purposes of
defense and promotion of the general welfare, is usually cited as the
basis for the federal role in education.

By means of a number of important pieces of legislation—the
Northwest Ordinance of 1785, the Morrill Land-Grant Act of 1862, the
Smith-Hughes Act of 1917, the Servicemen's Readjustment Act of 1944
(the "G.I. Bill of Rights"), the National Defense Education Act of 1958,
and the Elementary and Secondary Education Act of 1965—the federal
government has had a vital influence on American education. Most
education legislation has taken the form of categorial aid for specific
purposes rather than general aid.

The chief educational agency of the federal government is the
Office of Education (USOE), although it should be noted that educational programs and provisions are not confined to this agency. Less
than half of the federal expenditures for education are made by the
USOE; the rest is divided among a welter of agencies: the Office of
Economic Opportunity, the Office of Emergency Planning, the Atomic
Energy Commission, the Office of Science and Technology, the Smith-
sonian Institution, the National Foundation on the Arts and Humani-
ties, and the Central Intelligence Agency.

Historically, the USOE has not had much power or status. Its legal
basis was laid in 1867; subsequently it was renamed Bureau of Education and that title was retained until 1929, when the present title was
restored. More significantly, the agency was part of the Department of
the Interior until 1939; it was then transferred to the Federal Security
Agency, where it remained until 1953, when it became part of the
newly established Department of Health, Education and Welfare. Some
educators still believe, however, that education does not receive sufficient recognition at the federal level, and therefore have proposed that
the Commissioner of Education be made a member of the President's
cabinet.

The original purpose of the USOE was the collection and distribution of statistics and other information about the nation's educational systems. This has continued to be a primary function of the USOE, but in recent years it has been augmented by the task of administering and distributing the growing amount of federal aid to education (for instance, while in 1957–58, 4 percent of public school revenues was received from the federal government; in 1968–69, the percentage had increased to 8 percent). Of this aid, the most important single act to date was the multibillion-dollar Elementary and Secondary Act of 1965, which, while providing support for many purposes and programs, earmarked most of the funds for upgrading the education of children from low-income families.

One would be remiss, however, to overlook the vital role of the Supreme Court in shaping educational policy. In fact, it can plausibly be argued that no other body, with the exception of certain states, has influenced educational policy so significantly. From its desegregation decisions beginning with the *Brown* case in 1954 to its many decisions on church-state relations in education to its other vital decisions on academic freedom, loyalty, and censorship, the influence of the Court has been felt in all sections of the land.[23] It should also be noted that the Court's decisions on the reapportionment of state legislatures (*Baker* v. *Carr*) and on congressional reapportionment (*Wesberry* v. *Sanders*) may ultimately have profound effects on education.

In examining the impact of national forces on local school systems, the importance of the National Education Association (NEA) and the American Federation of Teachers (AFT) should be considered. Although the NEA has not had as much influence with the Congress as, say, the American Medical Association, it has exerted influence in many other ways. It was earlier mentioned that the NEA has powerful state education associations in some sections of the country. Moreover, it has provided many services to teachers and administrators through its network of organizations that cater to more specialized interests. It has also had an impact through such important commissions as the Committee of Ten, the Commission on the Reorganization of Secondary Education, and the Educational Policies Commission.

The AFT has grown rapidly in numbers and strength during the past decade so that today it is a genuine force in competing for the loyalties of teachers in large metropolitan communities. It has exerted influence on local school boards by its vigorous stand on collective bargaining and its ability to organize teachers for concerted action. And it has competed very effectively with the NEA, especially in large city school districts, often moving the NEA from its more conservative stance to a stronger one in order to compete effectively. It remains an open question whether these two organizations, which are no longer so far apart in actual practice as they were fifteen years ago, will merge. To what extent such a merger would change the direction of educational policy is a vital question which remains open to speculation.

Several other influential forces are at work nationwide. Through public and private colleges and universities throughout the country, teachers and administrators are prepared for their positions in public and private school systems. Although each state establishes certification requirements with which teacher-education programs are expected to comply, these requirements still allow colleges considerable discretion in determining the education of teachers.

Some critics have charged that the preparation of public school personnel is largely in the hands of "educationists," and it is certainly evident that those who staff the schools and colleges of education are products of the same system. According to some critics, this reinforces the strength of the educational establishment, which is also made up of persons of similar outlooks, background, and training. For instance, the USOE, state departments of education, the NEA, and state teachers' associations are largely staffed by such persons (although this pattern changed somewhat for the USOE beginning with the administration of Sterling McMurrin in the early 1960s).[24] If these claims can actually be supported, then there surely is an interlocking establishment. However, in order to support the claims, a great deal of additional information would first be needed about the staffing of these different organizations and, it would be necessary to consider whatever diversity there is in teacher education. Finally, it would be necessary to examine the policy decisions of these different institutions and agencies to determine to what extent their decisions overlap, interlock, and reinforce one another. Until these factors are more carefully assessed, the claim remains only a plausible charge. However, if the charge were substantiated, the alleged interlocking nature of the establishment would, in concert, constitute the single most important and potent force acting on the American public schools.

Another nationwide influence that should not be ignored is the textbook industry and related media industries, which provide materials for schools throughout the nation. In view of the fact that most teachers still rely heavily on basic texts, this influence could be considerable. However, before too much importance is attached to publishers, one would first need to assume that only one point of view dominates the market, either because of a monopoly in the publishing industry or because the nation's schools essentially want one point of view presented. But since these assumptions are false, the influence exerted by the publishing and media industries on the schools, though important, is diverse and diffused. The situation is more uniform where a state textbook commission selects the approved texts for the state's public schools.

Testing companies, which produce standardized, machine-scored tests, also have had considerable impact on both schools and colleges. The College Board exams alone, administered through the Educational Testing Service, have exerted an incalculable influence on secondary schools and colleges. Many other types of tests—achievement tests, I.Q. tests, ability tests, personality, attitude, and interest inventories—have played a significant role in education at all levels. In spite of numerous criticisms and objections made over the years against various types of tests, many American educators have shown unbounded faith in the benefits of testing. This attitude is reinforced by business, industry, and government, which also widely utilize tests of their employees and information of test results (when such information is available) of high school and college graduates.

Higher education exerts influence on secondary schools in a number of ways, especially in terms of college-entrance requirements. A century ago, when only a small percentage of youth attended high school, many of those who did attend were interested in going on to college. During this century an increasingly larger proportion of the population graduated from high school; but in order to fulfill the interests and aspirations of these new secondary students, it was necessary to provide terminal vocational training. Today a majority of high school youth expect upon graduation to enter some form of higher or continuing education. Thus, the press of college-entrance requirements on the curriculum looms large once again. Public and private school curriculum policies have been shaped to a noticeable extent by these requirements.

The demands of business and industry for trained manpower have affected the types of vocational programs established by secondary schools. The schools have had to be attuned to market needs so that their graduates will be able to find a place for their skills. At the same time, there have been periods where a national trend for manpower could be observed. This trend was particularly evident during the late 1950s with the Russians' launching of *Sputnik* and the subsequent passage of the National Defense Education Act. The cry was for more scientists and mathematicians in order for the United States to keep up (or forge ahead) in the space race. Different priorities for the curriculum were set during the early 1960s with new programs in the sciences, mathematics, foreign languages, and other areas. In conclusion, local policy-makers usually attempt to be sensitive to manpower needs, although at times they may be shortsighted and ignore the need to prepare youth for a national job market rather than merely for local community conditions.

ESTABLISHING NEW RELATIONSHIPS IN EDUCATIONAL POLICY

We will consider two promising proposals for bringing about closer relationships among the local, state, and federal levels and creating more consistent and uniform policies. The first is James B. Conant's proposal for evolving a nationwide policy for education.[25] Conant holds that there will not be a national policy unless there is a constitutional amendment (and such an amendment policy, he believes, is highly unlikely); there can, however, be greater cooperative exploration by the states and the federal government. Accordingly, he has proposed that the states, or at least the fifteen or twenty most populous states, "enter into a compact for the creation of an 'Interstate Commission for Planning a Nationwide Educational Policy.' "[26] Parallels can be drawn with various commissions for fostering cooperation among institutions of higher education, such as the Western Interstate Commission for Higher Education (thirteen states) and the New England Board of Higher Education (six states).

The proposed commission would be responsible for drawing up plans rather than serving as a new administrative body. It would meet only periodically, while the actual work would be carried on by special committees. The commission would be empowered to gather important information about the education and subsequent employment of professional people in the various states, scholarship and loan programs for students, the location of centers for study beyond the bachelor's degree, the impact of federal spending on education, and other vital statistics. Conant believes there are a number of basic, widely shared beliefs or premises about education which could be adopted by the commission, and if every state legislature would pass a resolution approving these beliefs, we would for the first time have a nationwide policy. These premises center around such convictions as free schooling, the responsibility for educating the young to participate capably in a democracy, the right of parents to send their children to private schools, compulsory education, the need for educational opportunities beyond high school, vocational preparation, and the responsibility for financing education, including research in higher education. While it could be said, parenthetically, that these beliefs are probably held by a majority of the population, they are sufficiently general and global in character to be open to interpretation and debate. Nevertheless, these premises, whether fully accepted or not, do not seem to be a critical factor in Conant's proposal.

Conant's considerable influence in American education proved fruitful in 1966 (two years after the proposal was made) when the Compact for Education created the Education Commission of the States. The commission is composed of politicians, including governors, educators, and laymen; and almost all of the states have voluntarily joined it. The commission's activities have been diverse, but essentially the focus has been on federal-state relations. It is still too early to tell whether it will realize its possibilities of creating interstate and possibly nationwide policies.

Following Conant's proposal but prior to the formation of the commission, Roald Campbell and Gerald Sroufe presented another position on forging new federal-state-local relations.[27] They disagreed with Conant by presenting some telling arguments to show that, although there is no total national policy, national policy already exists. It can be found in such examples as the *Brown* decision and the National Defense Education Act. They argued that since there already are some nationwide policies and since improved education is also in the national interest, the framework for a partnership is and has been present for some time. By exploring the actions surrounding the Constitutional Convention and selected court decisions on the matter, they conclude that there is evidence of a partnership in almost all areas. This partnership, they contend, is likely to grow in future years; however, in order for it to be most fruitful, it should observe certain principles. These principles include utilizing the resources at all three levels in meeting educational problems. Second, each of the partners in this endeavor must be strong. The local level needs to consolidate school districts until there are about five thousand districts, while, at the same time, the largest metropolitan districts should be divided to keep education close to the people. Third, the states will need to provide more leadership. Fourth, the operations of schools, as far as possible, should be delegated to the local districts. Finally, the federal government should concern itself with national needs and should provide the financial aid to meet these needs.

The principles offered by Campbell and Sroufe seem unremarkable insofar as they have been stated in various forms before, and it is not altogether clear whether they will assure the development of the proposed partnership. On the other hand, the authors have clearly shown the extent of nationwide policy, which was glaringly overlooked by Conant. Since Conant's argument for the proposed commission rested largely on the alleged lack of such policy, it would seem that, theoretically speaking, the commission is superfluous. But in view of the fact that the commission has now been created, it would be unfair to make additional prejudicial statements before it has been given a chance to refute its detractors by demonstrating the importance of its activities.

In conclusion, it should be noted that some of the weaknesses of present-day policy-making stem from inadequate planning, lack of clear understanding of the nature of policy and its operations, an inability to plan intelligently for change, and a tendency to treat policy-making as essentially for the purpose of institutional maintenance rather than institutional renewal and reconstruction, which is due, at least in part, to the exclusive use of equilibrium and consensus models. It is hoped that some of the ideas presented in this book will at least mark a fresh beginning in the task of overcoming these problems and thereby give a sense of direction for the many creative and imaginative people who will be needed in reforming educational policy.

Notes

CHAPTER 1

1. Among the many important studies in this area are the following: C. I. Barnard, *The Functions of the Executive* (Cambridge: Harvard University Press, 1940); Peter M. Blau and W. Richard Scott, *Formal Organizations* (San Francisco: Chandler, 1962); Amitai Etzioni, *A Comparative Analysis of Complex Organizations* (Glencoe, Ill.: Free Press, 1961); James G. March and Herbert A. Simon, *Organizations* (New York: John Wiley, 1958); and F. J. Roethlisberger and W. J. Dickson, *Management and the Worker* (Cambridge: Harvard University Press, 1957).

2. See: Chris Argyris, *Personality and Organization* (New York: Harper & Brothers, 1957); and Abraham H. Maslow, *Eupsychian Management* (Homewood, Ill.: Richard D. Irwin, Dorsey Press, 1965).

3. See: Charles Bidwell, "Some Causes of Conflict and Tensions Among Teachers," *Administrators Notebook* 5 (March 1956); C. Wayne Gordon, *The Social System of the High School* (New York: Free Press, 1957); Gerald H. Moeller, "Bureaucracy and the Teacher's Sense of Power," *Administrators Notebook* 11 (November 1962); and Charles Page, "Bureaucracy and Higher Education," *Journal of General Education* 5 (1951): 91–100.

4. For a review of recent studies, see: Michael W. Kirst and Edith K. Mosher, "Politics of Education," *Review of Educational Research* 39 (December 1969): 623–41.

5. As examples: Theodore Powell, *The School Bus Law* (Middleton, Conn: Wesleyan University Press, 1960); Leo Pfeffer, *Church, State, and Freedom* (Boston: Beacon Press, 1953); James M. O'Neill, *Religion and Education Under the Constitution* (New York: Harper & Brothers, 1949); Alan Barth, *The Loyalty of Free Men* (New York: Viking Press, 1951); R. Freeman Butts, *The American Tradition in Religion and Education* (Boston: Beacon Press, 1950); Richard Hofstadter and Walter P. Metzger, *The Development of Academic Freedom in the United States* (New York: Columbia University Press, 1955).

6. Examples of policy studies in other disciplines: Raymond A. Bauer and Kenneth J. Garten, eds., *The Study of Policy Formation* (New York: Free Press, 1968); James Sundquist, *Politics and Policy* (Washington: Brookings Institution, 1968); Edmund P. Learned et al., *Business Policy: Texts and Cases* (Homewood, Ill.: Richard D. Irwin, 1965); Raymond A. Bauer et al., *American Business and*

Public Policy (New York: Atherton Press, 1963); and J. Robinson, *Congress and Foreign Policy-Making* (Homewood, Ill.: Dorsey Press, 1962).

CHAPTER 2

1. *Policy Making for American Public Schools* (New York: 1969), National Academy of Education, pp. 5–6.

2. Roald F. Campbell, John E. Corbally, Jr., and John A. Ramseyer, *Introduction to Educational Administration*, 3d ed. (Boston: Allyn & Bacon, 1967), p. 257.

3. John Walton, *Administration and Policy-Making in Education*, rev. ed. (Baltimore: Johns Hopkins University Press, 1969), pp. 52–53.

4. Raymond A. Bauer, "The Study of Policy Formation: An Introduction," in *The Study of Policy Formation*, ed. Raymond A. Bauer and Kenneth J. Gergen, (New York: Free Press, 1968). pp. 1–2.

5. Ibid., p. 2.

6. Stanley E. Ballinger, *The Nature and Function of Educational Policy* (Bloomington: Center for the Study of Educational Policy, Indiana University, May 1965), p. 4.

7. Jean Piaget, *The Moral Judgment of the Child* (New York: Free Press, 1965).

8. Walton, *Administration and Policy-Making*, pp. 52–61.

9. R. Bruce Raup et al., *The Improvement of Practical Intelligence* (New York: Bureau of Publications, Teachers College, Columbia University, 1950), chap. 5.

10. Ballinger, *Nature and Function of Educational Policy*, p. 5.

11. Irwin Bross, *Design for Decision* (New York: Macmillan, 1953), p.2.

12. R. D. Luce and Howard Raiffa, *Games and Decisions: Introduction and Critical Survey* (New York: John Wiley, 1957).

13. Ward Edwards, Harold Lindman, and Leonard J. Savage, "Bayesian Statistical Inference for Psychological Research," *Psychological Review* 70 (1963): 193–95.

14. P. M. Morse and G. E. Kimball, *Methods of Operations Research*, rev. ed. (New York: John Wiley, 1951).

15. C. West Churchman, "Science and Decision-Making," *Philosophy of Science* 23 (1956): 247.

16. Herbert A. Simon, " Theories of Decision-Making in Economic and Behavioral Sciences," *American Economic Review* 49 (June 1959): 277.

17. Martin Patchen, "Decision Theory in the Study of National Action: Problems and a Proposal," *Journal of Conflict Resolution* 9 (June 1965): 164–75. Patchen specifically recommends Atkinson's theory of motivation. See: J. W. Atkinson, *An Introduction to Motivation* (Princeton: Van Nostrand, 1964).

CHAPTER 3

1. Alfred North Whitehead, "Philosophy of Life" in *Twentieth Century Philosophy*, ed. Dagobert D. Runes (New York: Philosophical Library, 1947), p. 134.

2. John S. Brubacher, *Bases for Policy in Higher Education* (New York: McGraw-Hill, 1965), pp. 108–9.

3. Philip G. Smith, *Philosophy of Education: Introductory Studies* (New York: Harper & Row, 1964), p. 53. Other philosophers of education have concurred that there is no strict logical implication between a formal philosophy and educational practice. However, they have disagreed as to what type of relationship, if any, exists. Some suggest that the relationship may be either situational, psychological, or entirely indirect. Cf.: Joe R. Burnett, "Observations on the Logic Implications of Philosophic Theory for Educational Theory and Practice," *Educational Theory* 11 (April 1961): 65–70; Hobert W. Burns, "The Logic of Educational Implication," *Educational Theory* 12 (January 1962): 53–63; and Robert S. Guttchen, "The Quest for Necessity," *Educational Theory* 16 (April 1966): 128–34.

4. Smith, *Philosophy of Education*, pp. 54–56.

5. John Dewey, The Sources of a Science of Education (New York: Horace Liveright, 1939).

6. Ibid., p. 51.

7. Thomas J. Howell, "Philosophy and the Control of Educational Beliefs," in *Proceedings of Twentieth Annual Meeting of the Philosophy of Education Society,* ed. Hugh C. Black (Lawrence: University of Kansas, 1964), pp. 59–66.

8. D. B. Gowin, "Can Educational Theory Guide Practice?" *Educational Theory* 13 (January 1963): 6–12.

9. Henry J. Perkinson, "A Note On: 'Can Education Guide Practice?'" *Educational Theory* 14 (April 1964): 93–94.

10. D. B. Gowin, "Defects in the Doctrine of Educational Strategies," *Educational Theory* 14 (April 1964): 95–98.

11. George L. Newsome, Jr., "In What Sense Is Theory a Guide to Practice?" *Educational Theory* 14 (January 1964): 31–39.

CHAPTER 4

1. The length of time depends upon a number of factors, including types of organizations, purposes, resources, and abilities of the managerial staff.

2. See: David Braybrooke and C. E. Lindblom, *A Strategy for Decision* (New York: Free Press, 1963). The authors substitute for the rationalistic model a refined version of "disjointed incrementalism," which, they claim, is based more closely on the way policy is actually developed.

3. See: Michael B. Katz, *Class, Bureaucracy, and Schools* (New York: Frederick Praeger, 1971), p. 107.

4. Max Weber, *Essays in Sociology,* trans. and ed. H. Gerth and C. Wright Mills (New York: Oxford University Press, 1958); idem, *The Theory of Social and Economic Organization,* trans. A. M. Henderson and Talcott Parsons (New York: Free Press, 1957).

5. Among the numerous studies in this area are the following works: F. J. Roethlisberger and W. J. Dickson, *Management and the Worker* (Cambridge:

Harvard University Press, 1941); C. I. Barnard, *The Functions of the Executive* (Cambridge: Harvard University Press, 1940); Leon Festinger, Stanley Schachter, and Kurt Back, *Social Pressures in Informal Groups* (New York: Harper & Row, 1950); Elton Mayo, *The Social Problems of an Industrial Civilization* (Boston: Harvard Business School, 1945); and A. Zalesnik, C. R. Christensen, and F. J. Roethlisberger, *The Motivation, Productivity, and Satisfaction of Workers: A Prediction Study* (Boston: Division of Research, Harvard Business School, 1958).

6. M. Chester et. al., "The Principal's Role in Facilitating Innovation," *Theory Into Practice* 1 (1963): 2.

7. Alfred Kuhn, *The Study of Society: A Unified Approach* (Homewood, Ill.: Richard D. Irwin, Dorsey Press, 1963), chap. 22.

8. Generally speaking, sociologists would consider a number of these so-called organizations to be associations and interest groups rather than organizations (as Kuhn would classify them).

9. Peter M. Blau and W. Richard Scott, *Formal Organizations: A Comparative Approach* (San Francisco: Chandler, 1962), p. 43.

10. Weber, *Theory of Social and Economic Organization*, p. 328. Weber also discusses traditional authority and charismatic authority, neither of which is of direct concern for analyzing authority structures in bureaucracies.

11. Ibid., p. 152.

12. This point is made by S. I. Benn and R. S. Peters, who contrast de jure and de facto concepts of authority. See their *The Principles of Political Thought* (New York: Free Press, 1959), pp. 20, 352.

13. Peter Schrag, *Village School Downtown* (Boston: Beacon Press, 1968), pp. 14–15.

14. David Rogers, *110 Livingston Street* (New York: Vintage Books, 1969).

15. Two recent examples of superintendents hired for this purpose were in Louisville and Philadelphia. See: Peter Binzen, "Philadelphia: Politics Invades the Schools," *Saturday Review*, February 5, 1972, pp. 44–49; Terry Borton, "Reform Without Politics in Louisville," *Saturday Review*, February 5, 1972, pp. 51–55.

16. Amitai Etzioni, *A Comparative Analysis of Complex Organizations* (Glencoe, Ill.: Free Press, 1961).

17. Warren A. Hughes, *Statistics of Local Public School Systems, Fall 1969: Pupils and Staff* (Washington: U.S. Department of Health, Education and Welfare, 1971).

18. Ernest Dale, *Planning and Developing the Company Organization Structure* (New York: American Management Association, 1955), p. 112.

19. Peter M. Blau, *The Dynamics of Bureaucracy* (Chicago: University of Chicago Press, 1955).

20. Harold H. Kelley, "Communication in Experimentally Created Hierarchies," *Human Relations* 4 (1951): 39–56.

21. John I. Goodlad, M. Frances Klein, and associates *Behind the Classroom Door* (Worthington, Ohio: Charles A. Jones, 1970), p. 41.

22. See: Raymond E. Callahan, *The Cult of Efficiency* (Chicago: University of Chicago Press, 1962).

23. Lewis A. Coser has shown that such figures as Talcott Parsons, George A. Lundberg, Elton Mayo, and W. Lloyd Warner and Kurt Lewin have neglected the study of social conflict. See Coser's *The Function of Social Conflict* (Glencoe, Ill.: Free Press, 1956), pp. 20–26.

24. An exception to this trend is found in "The Organizational Roots of Discord," chap. 8 in Ronald G. Corwin's *Militant Professionalism* (New York: Appleton-Century-Crofts, 1970), pp. 203–42.

25. Coser, *Functions of Social Conflict*, p. 8.

26. Ibid.

27. Schrag, *Village School Downtown*, pp. 54, 57, 75.

28. Rogers, *110 Livingston Street*, pp. 286–87.

29. Lloyd K. Bishop, *Individualizing Educational Systems* (New York: Harper & Row, 1971), chap. 12.

30. Ibid.

31. Bennis's writings on this topic include *Changing Organizations* (New York: McGraw-Hill, 1966); *American Bureaucracy* (Chicago: Aldine, 1970), pp. 3–16, 165–87; "Leadership Theory and Administrative Behavior," *Administrative Science Quarterly*, 4, No. 3 (December 1959): 259–301.

32. Bishop, *Individualizing Educational Systems*, chap. 13.

33. Francis S. Chase, "The Teacher and Policy Making," *Administrator's Notebook* 1, no. 1 (May 1952).

CHAPTER 5

1. David Braybrooke and Charles E. Lindblom, *A Strategy of Decision* (New York: Free Press, 1970), chap. 1 and 2.

2. Ibid., chap. 4.

3. Ibid., chap. 5.

4. It is not our purpose to take up various techniques of research. The interested reader should consult such works as: Fred N. Kerlinger, *Foundations of Behavioral Research* (New York: Holt, Rinehart & Winston, 1964); and George J. Mouly, *The Science of Educational Research*, 2d ed. (New York: Van Nostrand Reinhold, 1970).

5. Stephen K. Bailey, *The Office of Education and the Education Act of 1965*, Inter-University Case Program (Indianapolis: Bobbs-Merrill, 1966).

6. George S. Counts, *The Social Composition of School Boards*, University of Chicago Supplementary Monographs, no. 33 (Chicago, 1937).

7. W. Lloyd Warner, Robert J. Havighurst, and Martin B. Loeb, *Who shall Be Educated?* (New York: Harper & Row, 1944), p. 101.

8. August B. Hollingshead, *Elmtown's Youth* (New York: John Wiley, 1949), pp. 122–26.

9. Roy M. Caughran, "The School Board Member Today," *American School Board Journal* 133 (November 1956): 39 and (December 1956): 26.

10. Roald F. Campbell, "Are School Boards Reactionary?" *Phi Delta Kappan* 27 (1945): 82–83, 93.

11. Herbert H. Hyman and Paul B. Sheatsley, "Attitudes toward Desegregation," *Scientific American* 195 (December 1956): 35–39.

12. Reinhard Bendix and Seymour M. Lipset, "Political Sociology: An Essay and Bibliography," *Current Sociology*, 6 (1957): 79–169.

13. Raymond E. Callahan, *Education and the Cult of Efficiency* (Chicago: University of Chicago Press, 1962).

14. Neal Gross, *Who Runs Our Schools?* (New York: John Wiley, 1958), chap. 7.

15. The most famous study representing this position at the community level is Floyd Hunter's *Community Power Structure* (Chapel Hill: University of North Carolina Press, 1953). C. Wright Mills shows an interlocking power structure at the national level in his *The Power Elite* (New York: Oxford University Press, 1956).

16. The pluralistic position is represented by Robert A. Dahl's *Who Governs?* (New Haven: Yale University Press, 1961).

17. Warner Bloomberg, Jr. and Morris Sunshine, *Suburban Power Structures and Public Education* (Syracuse, N. Y.: Syracuse University Press, 1963), chap. 5.

18. Warner, Havighurst, and Loeb, *Who Shall Be Educated?* Hubert P. Beck, *Men Who Control Universities* (New York: Kings Crown, 1947).

19. Reported in *Change* 4 (February 1972): 24.

20. See: James Bryant Conant, *Shaping Educational Policy* (New York: McGraw-Hill, 1964), chap. 2; and James D. Koerner, *Who Controls American Education?* (Boston: Beacon Press, 1968), chap. 4.

21. Conant, *Shaping Educational Policy*, p. 28.

22. Koerner, *Who Controls American Education?*, pp. 55–56.

23. For the text of some of the Supreme Court's decisions, see: Sam Duker, *The Public School and Religion* (New York: Harper & Row, 1966); Herbert M. Kliebard, ed., *Religion and Education in America: A Documentary History* (Scranton: International Textbook Co., 1969); and David Feldman, ed., *The Supreme Court and Education* (New York: Bureau of Publications, Teachers College, Columbia University, 1960).

24. See: Conant, *Shaping Educational Policy;* idem, *The Education of American Teachers* (New York: McGraw-Hill, 1963); Koerner, *Who Controls American Education?* idem, *The Miseducation of American Teachers* (Boston: Houghton Mifflin, 1963).

25. Conant, *Shaping Educational Policy*, chap. 5.

26. Ibid., p. 123.

27. Roald F. Campbell and Gerald E. Sroufe, "Toward A Rationale for Federal-State-Local Relations in Education," *Phi Delta Kappan* 47 (September 1965): 2–7.

Suggested Readings

CHAPTERS 1–3

BALLINGER, STANLEY E. "The Nature and Function of Educational Policy." Occasional Paper No. 65–101. Center for the Study of Educational Policy. Bloomington, Ind.: Indiana University Press, 1965.

BAUER, RAYMOND A., and GERGEN, KENNETH J., eds. *The Study of Policy Formation.* New York: Free Press, 1968.

BRAYBROOKE, DAVID, and LINDBLOM, CHARLES E. *A Strategy for Decision.* New York: Free Press, 1963.

DROR, YEHEZKEL. *Public Policymaking Reexamined.* San Francisco: Chandler, 1968.

LEYS, WAYNE A. R. *Ethics for Policy Decisions.* Englewood Cliffs, N.J.: Prentice-Hall, 1952.

LINDBLOM, CHARLES E. *The Policy-Making Process.* Englewood Cliffs, N.J.: Prentice-Hall, 1968.

McLURE, WILLIAM P., and MILLER, VAN, eds. *Government of Public Education for Adequate Policy Making.* Urbana, Ill.: Bureau of Educational Research, University of Illinois, 1960.

RAUP, R. BRUCE, et al. *The Improvement of Practical Intelligence.* New York: Bureau of Publications, Teachers College, Columbia University, 1950.

SIMON, HERBERT A. *Administrative Behavior.* New York: Macmillan, 1955.

VIKERS, GEOFFREY. *The Art of Judgment.* New York: Basic Books, 1965.

WALTON, JOHN. *Administration and Policy-Making in Education.* Baltimore: Johns Hopkins University Press, 1969.

CHAPTER 4

BAILEY, STEPHEN K. *ESEA—The Office of Education Administers Law.* Syracuse, N.Y.: Syracuse University Press, 1968.

———, et al. *Schoolmen and Politics.* Syracuse, N.Y.: Syracuse University Press, 1962.

BLOOMBERG, WARNER, JR., and SUNSHINE, MORRIS. *Suburban Power Structures and Public Education.* Syracuse, N.Y.: Syracuse University Press, 1963.

BRAYBROOKE, DAVID, and LINDBLOM, CHARLES E. *A Strategy of Decision.* New York: Free Press, 1970.

CAHILL, ROBERT S., and HENCLEY, STEPHEN P., eds. *The Politics of Education in the Local Community.* Danville, Ill.: Interstate, 1964.

CAMPBELL, ROALD F.; CUNNINGHAM, LUVERN L.; and McPHEE, RODERICK F. *The Organization and Control of American Education.* Columbus: Charles E. Merrill, 1963.

CAMPBELL, ROALD F., and SROUFE, GERALD E. "Toward A Rationale for Federal-State-Local Relations in Education." *Phi Delta Kappan* 47 (September 1965): 2–7.

CAUGHRAN, ROY M. "The School Board Member Today." *American School Board Journal* 133 (November 1956): 39, and (December 1956): 26.

CHARTERS, W. W., JR. "Social Class Analysis and the Control of Public Education." *Harvard Educational Review* 23 (Fall 1953): 268–83.

CONANT, JAMES BRYANT. *Shaping Educational Policy.* New York: McGraw-Hill, 1964.

DAHL, ROBERT A. *Who Governs?* New Haven: Yale University Press, 1961.

GROSS, NEAL. *Who Runs Our Schools?* New York: John Wiley, 1958.

HUNTER, FLOYD. *Community Power Structure.* Chapel Hill: University of North Carolina Press, 1953.

KIMBROUGH, RALPH B. *Political Power and Educational Decision Making.* Chicago: Rand McNally, 1964.

LIPPITT, RONALD; WATSON, J.; and WESLEY, B. *The Dynamics of Planned Change.* 2d ed. New York: Holt, Rinehart & Winston, 1969.

MASTERS, NICHOLAS A., et al. *State Politics and Public Schools.* New York: Alfred A. Knopf, 1964.

MUNGER, FRANK J., and FENNO, RICHARD F., JR. *National Politics and Federal Aid to Education.* Syracuse, N.Y.: Syracuse University Press, 1962.

ROSENTHAL, ALAN, ed. *Governing Education.* Garden City, N.Y.: Doubleday, 1969.

CHAPTER 5

ANDERSON, JAMES G. *Bureaucracy in Education.* Baltimore: Johns Hopkins University Press, 1968.

BENNIS, WARREN G. *Changing Organizations.* New York: McGraw-Hill, 1966.

BISHOP, LLOYD K. *Individualizing Educational Systems.* New York: Harper & Row, 1971.

BLAU, PETER M., and SCOTT, W. RICHARD. *Formal Organizations.* San Francisco: Chandler, 1962.

BURKHEAD, JESSE. *Input and Output in Large-City High Schools.* Syracuse, N.Y.: Syracuse University Press, 1967.

CALLAHAN, RAYMOND E. *Education and the Cult of Efficiency.* Chicago: University of Chicago Press, 1962.

CORWIN, RONALD G. *Militant Professionalism.* New York: Appleton-Century-Crofts, 1970.

COSER, LEWIS A. *The Functions of Social Conflict.* New York: Free Press, 1956.

ETZIONI, AMITAI, ed. *Complex Organizations: A Sociological Reader.* New York: Holt, Rinehart & Winston, 1961.

———. *Modern Organizations.* Englewood Cliffs, N.J.: Prentice-Hall, 1964.

HAVIGHURST, ROBERT J. *The Public Schools of Chicago: A Survey for the Board of Education of the City of Chicago.* Chicago: Board of Education of the City of Chicago, 1964.

HOROWITZ, IRVING LOUIS. "Consensus, Conflict and Cooperation: A Sociological Inventory." *Social Forces* 41 (1962): 177–88.

KATZ, FRED E. "The School as a Complex Organization." *Harvard Educational Review* 34 (Summer 1964): 428–55.

KATZ, MICHAEL B. *Class, Bureaucracy, and Schools.* New York: Praeger, 1971.

MARCH, JAMES G., ed. *Handbook of Organizations.* Chicago: Rand McNally, 1966.

———, and SIMON, HERBERT A. *Organizations.* New York: John Wiley, 1958.

OWENS, ROBERT G. *Organizational Behavior in Schools.* Englewood Cliffs, N.J.: Prentice-Hall, 1970.

PEABODY, ROBERT L. *Organizational Authority.* New York: Atherton Press, 1964.

PRESTHUS, ROBERT. *The Organizational Society.* New York: Alfred A. Knopf, 1962.

ROGERS, DAVID. *110 Livingston Street.* New York: Vintage Books, 1969.

SCHRAG, PETER. *Village School Downtown.* Boston: Beacon Press, 1968.

WEBER, MAX. *The Theory of Social and Economic Organization.* Translated by A. M. Henderson and Talcott Parsons. New York: Free Press, 1957.